Oxford
International
Primary
Atlas

Editorial Adviser
Dr Patrick Wiegand

OXFORD
UNIVERSITY PRESS

Great Clarendon Street, Oxford OX2 6DP
Oxford University Press is a department of the University of Oxford.
It furthers the University's objective of excellence in research, scholarship,
and education by publishing worldwide in

Oxford   New York

Auckland   Cape Town   Dar es Salaam   Hong Kong   Karachi
Kuala Lumpur   Madrid   Melbourne   Mexico City   Nairobi
New Delhi   Shanghai   Taipei   Toronto

With offices in

Argentina   Austria   Brazil   Chile   Czech Republic   France   Greece
Guatemala   Hungary   Italy   Japan   Poland   Portugal   Singapore
South Korea   Switzerland   Thailand   Turkey   Ukraine   Vietnam

Oxford is a registered trade mark of Oxford University Press
in the UK and in certain other countries

ISBN: 978 0 19 848022 8

7 9 10 8

Printed in Singapore by KHL Printing Co. Pte Ltd.

D1611125

Acknowledgements

The publisher and authors would like to thank the following:

P5r John Tomaselli/Alamy; **P5l** PlanetObserver/Science Photo Library; **P8t** Robert Harding Picture Library Ltd/Alamy; **P8tc** The Photolibrary Wales/Alamy; **P8c** geogphotos/Alamy; **P8bc** Ivan J Belcher/Worldwide Picture Library/Alamy; **P8b** Chinch Gryniewicz/Ecoscene/Corbis; **P9tr** Jonathan Dorey - Scotland/Alamy; **P9tl** Britain On View/Photolibrary.com; **P9bl** Graham Oliver/Alamy; **P9br** Realimage/Alamy; **P10tl** Kevin Allen/Alamy; **P10tr** Peter Harrison/Photolibrary.com; **P10br** Travel Pix/Robert Harding Travel/Photolibrary.com; **P10bl** Carole Castelli/Shutterstock; **P11tr** /NASA; **P11tl** Planetary Visions Ltd/Science Photo Library; **P11bl** NASA/age fotostock/Photolibrary.com; **P11br** /NASA; **P12-13** PlanetObserver/Science Photo Library; **P16** Peter Adams/The Image Bank/Getty Images; **P17tr** Igor Plotnikov/Shutterstock; **P17bl** NPA/Stone/Getty Images; **P17br** Image Makers/The Image Bank/Getty Images; **P20cl** mediacolor's/Alamy; **P20tl** Radius Images/Photolibrary.com; **P20tr** Ron Watts/Corbis; **P20bl** ashfordplatt/Alamy; **P20br** Charles & Josette Lenars/Corbis; **P21tl** John Warburton-Lee/Photolibrary.com; **P21tr** Richard A. Cooke/Corbis; **P21bl** Wolfgang Kaehler/Corbis; **P21bc** Galen Rowell/Terra/Corbis; **P21br** Frans Lemmens/The Image Bank/Getty Images; **P22l** Jan Krimmer/imagebroker.net/Photolibrary.com; **P22r** Christian Heinrich/imagebroker RF/Photolibrary.com; **P23bl** Ben Osborne/Stone/Getty Images; **P23br** Faw... **P23t** Neale Clarke/Robert Harding Travel/Photolibrary.com; **P24** Claud... **P30bl** Ingolf Pompe 5/Alamy; **P30br** Simon Margetson/Alamy; **P30cr**... David Ball/Terra/Corbis; **P32** mikeuk/iStockphoto.com; **P35t** Joel Saget... Pepeira Tom/Iconotec/Photolibrary.com; **P37br** Superstock/Photolibra... **P37t** Albert Kerstna/iStockphoto.com; **P39t** Kristian Peetz/Shutterstoc... Photolibrary.com; **P39br** Josef Beck/imagebroker.net/Photolibrary.com... iStockphoto.com; P41t David Trood/The Image Bank/Getty Images; **P4**... Image/Science Photo Library; **P43t** yanta/iStockphoto.com; **P43b** John...

Press/Rex Features; **P47b** Tim Wright/Alamy; **P48** Jagadeesh/Reuters/Corbis; **P51** Emma Sklar/Rex Features; **P52** Robert Francis/Robert Harding Travel/Photolibrary.com; **P53** Peter Parks/AFP/Getty Images; **P57tl** Gregory Dimijian/Science Photo Library; **P57tr** Tom Brakefield/Flirt/Corbis; **P57bl** Keith Shuttlewood/Alamy; **P57br** Lite Productions/Photolibrary.com; **P58** Yann Arthus-Bertrand/ Encyclopedia/Corbis; **P59** Alex Bartel/Digital Light Source/Peter Arnold/Still Pictures; **P63** James Randklev/Photographer's Choice/Getty Images; **P64r** Don Hebert/Taxi/Getty Images; **P64l** Alvaro Leiva/age fotostock/Photolibrary.com; **P65t** Jane Sweeney/Encyclopedia/Corbis; **P65b** Frans Lanting/Latitude/Corbis; **P69l** Pascal Rondeau/Stone/Getty Images; **P69c** Julia Rogers/Alamy; **P69r** Thomas Schmitt/The Image Bank/Getty Images; **P70** Pete Niesen/Shutterstock; **P71l** Chris McLennan/Photolibrary.com; **P71c** John Lamb/Stone/Getty Images; **P71r** Chris Ballentine/Paul Thompson Images/Alamy; **P72t** Zeebra/Cusp/Corbis; **P72c** Paul A. Souders/Encyclopedia/Corbis; **P72b** Wildtrack Media/Rex Features; **P74t** Roberto Rinaldi/Tips Italia/Photolibrary.com; **P74bl** Calvin W Hall/Alaskastock/Photolibrary.com; **P74br** Keith Levit Photography/Photolibrary.com; **P75t** Robert Harding Picture Library Ltd/Alamy; **P75bl** Galen Rowell/Corbis; **P75br** Fritz Polking/ ...ages/Photolibrary.com.

...by Suzanne Williams/Pictureresearch.co.uk

...y:
...18 (icons); Mark Duffin p5 (compass), Gary Hincks p8, p9; Harry Venning p18

...Cliff Wassmann/iStockphoto. Cover globe by Jan Rysavy/iStockphoto

2 Contents

World

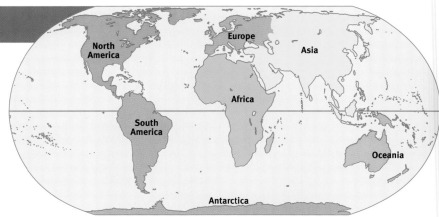

Europe

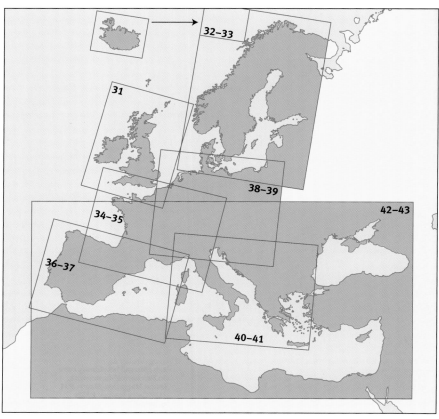

Contents 3

Asia

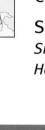

South America

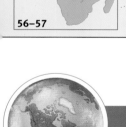

Africa

Oceania

North America

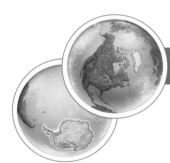

The Poles

© Oxford University Press

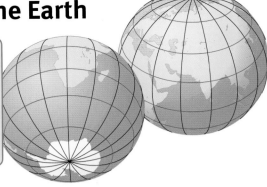

○ The Earth is a planet in space. It is a sphere. Two sets of imaginary lines help us describe where places are on the surface of the Earth.

Latitude

Lines of latitude measure distance north or south of the equator.

The **Equator** is at latitude 0°.

The **Poles** are at latitude 90°N and 90°S.

Can you find the **Equator**, the **Prime Meridian** and the **International Date Line** on a globe? **?**

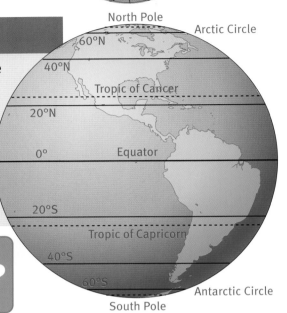

North Pole
Arctic Circle
60°N
40°N
Tropic of Cancer
20°N
0° Equator
20°S
Tropic of Capricorn
40°S
60°S
Antarctic Circle
South Pole

Longitude

Lines of longitude measure distance east or west of the Prime Meridian.

The **Prime Meridian** (also called the Greenwich Meridian) is at longitude 0°.

The **International Date Line** (on the other side of the Earth) is based on longitude 180°.

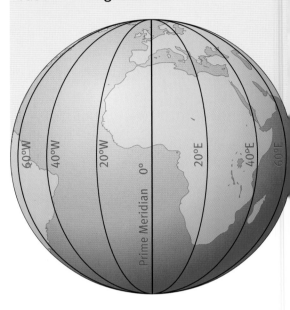

60°W 40°W 20°W Prime Meridian 0° 20°E 40°E 60°E

○ There are many ways of showing the spherical Earth on a flat world map.

Map projections

How a world map looks depends on where it is going to be used.

World map used in Europe and Africa

World map used in Australia and New Zealand

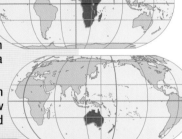

Can you find Antarctica on a globe and compare how it looks on a world map? **?**

Grid codes

In this atlas, the lines of latitude and longitude are used to make a grid.

The columns of the grid have letters.

The rows of the grid have numbers.

Numbers and letters together make a **grid code** that can be used to describe where places are on the Earth.

Can you name the city at gridcode **B2**? **?**

Casablanca
MOROCCO
Tripoli
Cairo
EGYPT
MEDITERRANEAN SEA
Tropic of Cancer
ALGERIA
LIBYA
MALI
NIGER
CHAD
Khartoum
SUDAN
SOUTH SUDAN
ETHIOPIA
Abuja
Monrovia
Mogadishu
KENYA
Equator
DEMOCRATIC REPUBLIC OF CONGO
TANZANIA
Dodoma
INDIAN OCEAN
ATLANTIC OCEAN
Luanda
ANGOLA
ZAMBIA
MADAGASCAR
Tropic of Capricorn
NAMIBIA
BOTSWANA
REPUBLIC OF SOUTH AFRICA
Durban
Cape Town
SOUTHERN OCEAN
Prime Meridian

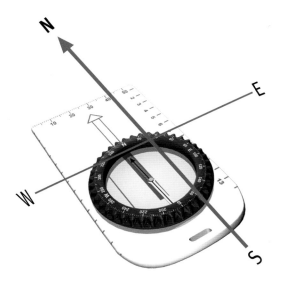

A compass is used for finding direction. The needle of a compass always points north.

Which way is North?

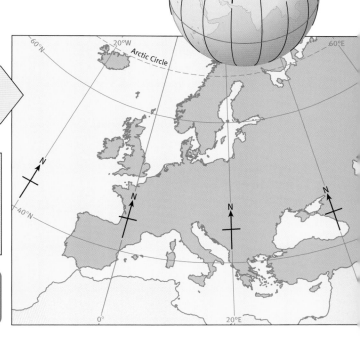

North on atlas maps follows the lines of longitude.

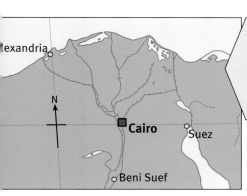

Cairo is **north** of Beni Suef.

Beni Suef is **south** of Cairo.

Suez is **east** of Cairo.

Alexandria is **north west** of Cairo.

Using a compass, can you find which direction north is from where you are?

Global Positioning System (GPS) satellites send signals to equipment on the ground. When a GPS receiver, such as SatNav in a car, picks up signals from several satellites it can work out where it is and give directions to where you want to go.

How does SatNav work?

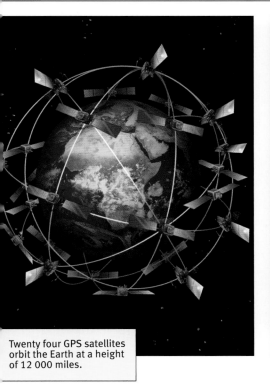

Twenty four GPS satellites orbit the Earth at a height of 12 000 miles.

A SatNav receiver has to be able to 'see' at least four satellites to work out where it is.

Tell SatNav where you want to go and it gives you directions. This one has a moving map as well as voice instructions.

6 Understanding maps

◎ Special words are used to describe parts of maps.

Map language

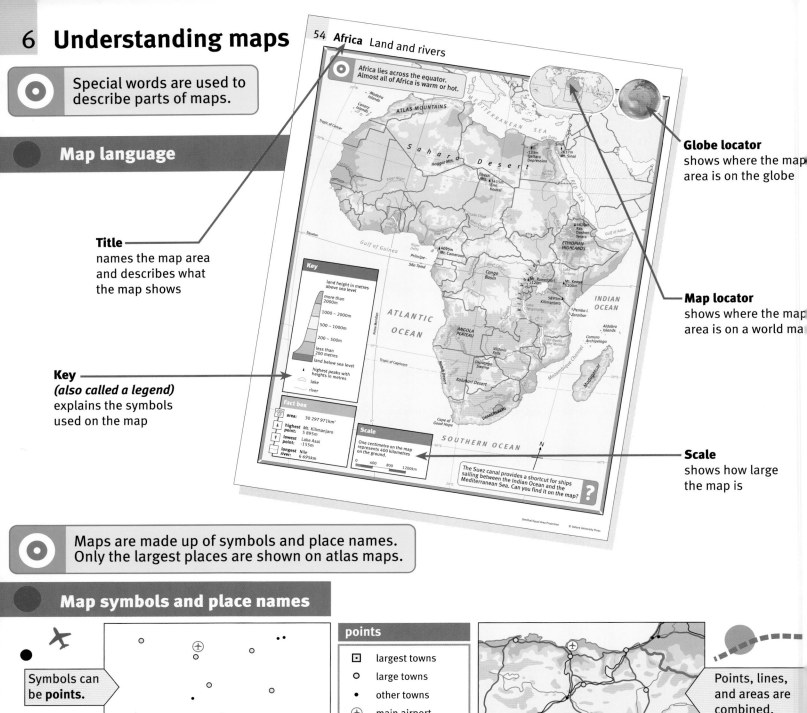

Africa Land and rivers

Africa lies across the equator. Almost all of Africa is warm or hot.

Title
names the map area and describes what the map shows

Key
(also called a legend)
explains the symbols used on the map

Globe locator
shows where the map area is on the globe

Map locator
shows where the map area is on a world map

Scale
shows how large the map is

The Suez canal provides a shortcut for ships sailing between the Indian Ocean and the Mediterranean Sea. Can you find it on the map?

◎ Maps are made up of symbols and place names. Only the largest places are shown on atlas maps.

Map symbols and place names

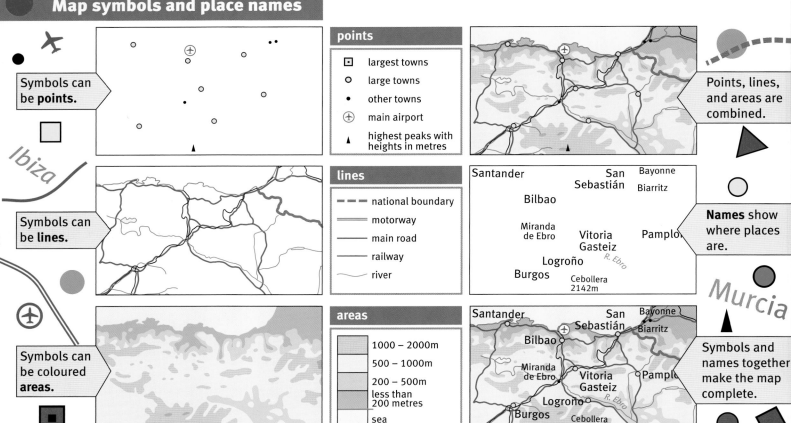

Symbols can be **points**.

Symbols can be **lines**.

Symbols can be coloured **areas**.

points
- ⊡ largest towns
- ○ large towns
- • other towns
- ⊕ main airport
- ▲ highest peaks with heights in metres

lines
- - - - national boundary
- ═══ motorway
- ─── main road
- ─── railway
- ～～ river

areas
- 1000 – 2000m
- 500 – 1000m
- 200 – 500m
- less than 200 metres
- sea

Santander   San Sebastián   Bayonne
Bilbao   Biarritz
Miranda de Ebro   Vitoria Gasteiz   Pamplo
Logroño   R. Ebro
Burgos   Cebollera 2142m

Santander   San Sebastián   Bayonne
Bilbao   Biarritz
Miranda de Ebro   Vitoria Gasteiz   Pampl
Logroño   R. Ebro
Burgos   Cebollera ▲2142m

Points, lines, and areas are combined.

Names show where places are.

Symbols and names together make the map complete.

© Oxford University Press

The way names are printed on maps gives an important clue to what sorts of places they describe.

Type on maps

North Island	South Island	Stewart Island	islands
NEW ZEALAND			countries
SOUTHERN ALPS	*Canterbury Plains*		land
River Wairau	*Lake Taupo*	*Hawke Bay*	water
Mt. Cook			mountain peaks
SOUTH PACIFIC OCEAN	*TASMAN SEA*		sea areas
Wellington	Auckland	Queenstown	settlements

An abbreviation is a shortened version of a word or a group of words.

R.	River
Mt.	Mount
Is.	Islands
Pen.	Peninsula

Map abbreviations

Some country names are abbreviated using the first letters of each word

UK	United Kingdom
USA	United States of America
UAE	United Arab Emirates

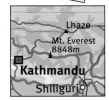

Atlas maps are much, much smaller than the places they show. A few centimetres on the map stand for very many kilometres on the ground.

Scale

Each division on the scale line is one centimetre. The scale line shows how many kilometres are represented by one centimetre.

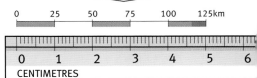

Scale

One centimetre on the map represents **60** kilometres on the ground.

0 60 120 180km

The distance between London and Reading is about 60km

Scale

One centimetre on the map represents **150** kilometres on the ground.

0 150 300 450km

The distance between San Diego and Los Angeles is about 150km

Scale

One centimetre on the map represents **550** kilometres on the ground.

0 550 1100 1650km

The distance between Bangkok and Yangon is about 550km

0 25 50 75 100 125km

0 1 2 3 4 5 6
CENTIMETRES

Larger scale smaller area more detail

Smaller scale larger area less detail

Choose a map from this atlas. Can you use a ruler to work out the distance in kilometres between two places? **?**

On atlas maps the height of the land is shown by colours.

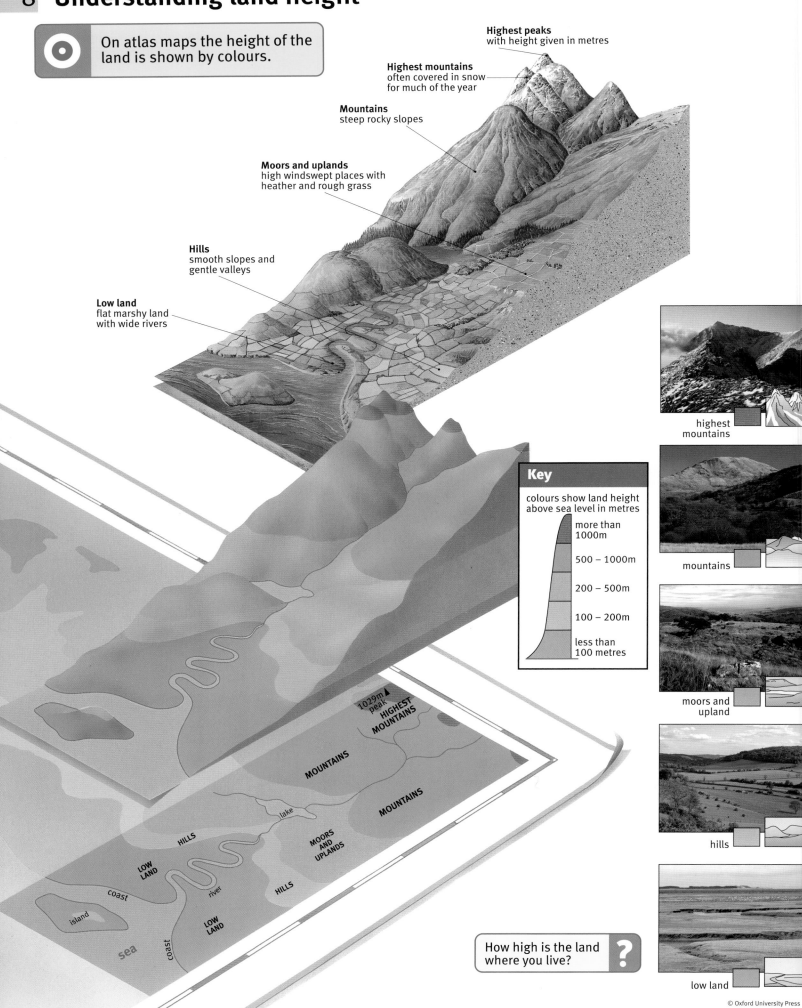

Highest peaks
with height given in metres

Highest mountains
often covered in snow
for much of the year

Mountains
steep rocky slopes

Moors and uplands
high windswept places with
heather and rough grass

Hills
smooth slopes and
gentle valleys

Low land
flat marshy land
with wide rivers

highest mountains

mountains

moors and upland

hills

low land

Key

colours show land height
above sea level in metres

more than 1000m

500 – 1000m

200 – 500m

100 – 200m

less than 100 metres

1029m peak

HIGHEST MOUNTAINS

MOUNTAINS

MOUNTAINS

lake

MOORS AND UPLANDS

HILLS

HILLS

LOW LAND

LOW LAND

coast

river

island

sea

coast

How high is the land where you live? **?**

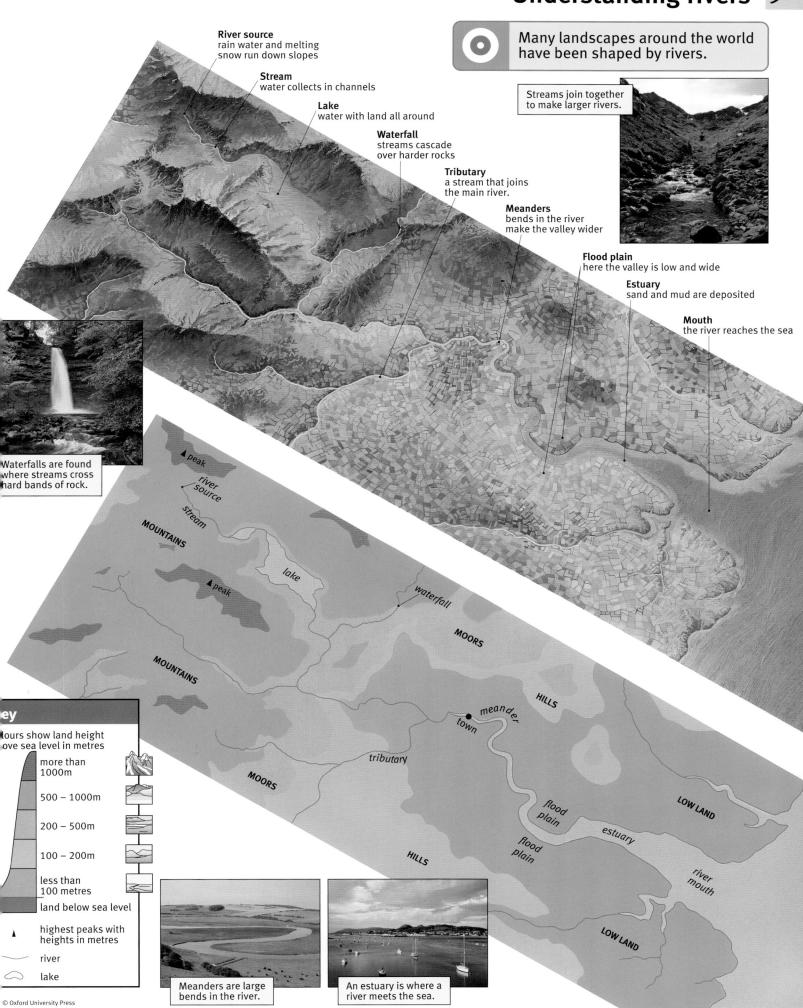

Many landscapes around the world have been shaped by rivers.

River source
rain water and melting snow run down slopes

Stream
water collects in channels

Lake
water with land all around

Waterfall
streams cascade over harder rocks

Tributary
a stream that joins the main river.

Meanders
bends in the river make the valley wider

Flood plain
here the valley is low and wide

Estuary
sand and mud are deposited

Mouth
the river reaches the sea

Streams join together to make larger rivers.

Waterfalls are found where streams cross hard bands of rock.

peak

river source

stream

MOUNTAINS

lake

waterfall

MOORS

peak

MOUNTAINS

HILLS

town

meander

tributary

MOORS

flood plain

LOW LAND

flood plain

estuary

HILLS

river mouth

LOW LAND

Key

Colours show land height above sea level in metres

more than 1000m

500 – 1000m

200 – 500m

100 – 200m

less than 100 metres

land below sea level

highest peaks with heights in metres

river

lake

Meanders are large bends in the river.

An estuary is where a river meets the sea.

People live in settlements of different sizes. More than half the world's people live in towns and cities.

Largest towns
o Very tall office buildings mark the centre of the largest towns.

Capital cities
■ The capital city is the most important city in a country. It is where the government meets.

Small towns and villages
Very small towns and villages are not shown on atlas maps. This village is Belmont-sur-Rance, northwest of Montpellier, France.

Other large towns
• Larger settlements have more shops and services than smaller ones.

What size of settlement do you live in?

Satellite images are pictures of the Earth taken from space. They help us understand the weather, our environment and the Earth itself.

Hundreds of working satellites orbit the Earth. There are also thousands that don't work any more, called 'space junk'.

Satellite images can show the movement of hurricanes and give warning to people who live in their path. This image shows Hurricane Katrina, one of the deadliest hurricanes ever. Compare this image with the map on page 60.

A snow-covered volcano explodes in the Aleutian Islands, Alaska. The cloud of ash was three miles high. Can you find the Aleutian Islands on the world map on page 16?

Satellites can measure changes in the temperature of the Earth. This image of Antarctica shows where the ice is melting. Red shows where the ice is melting most. Compare this satellite image with the map on page 75.

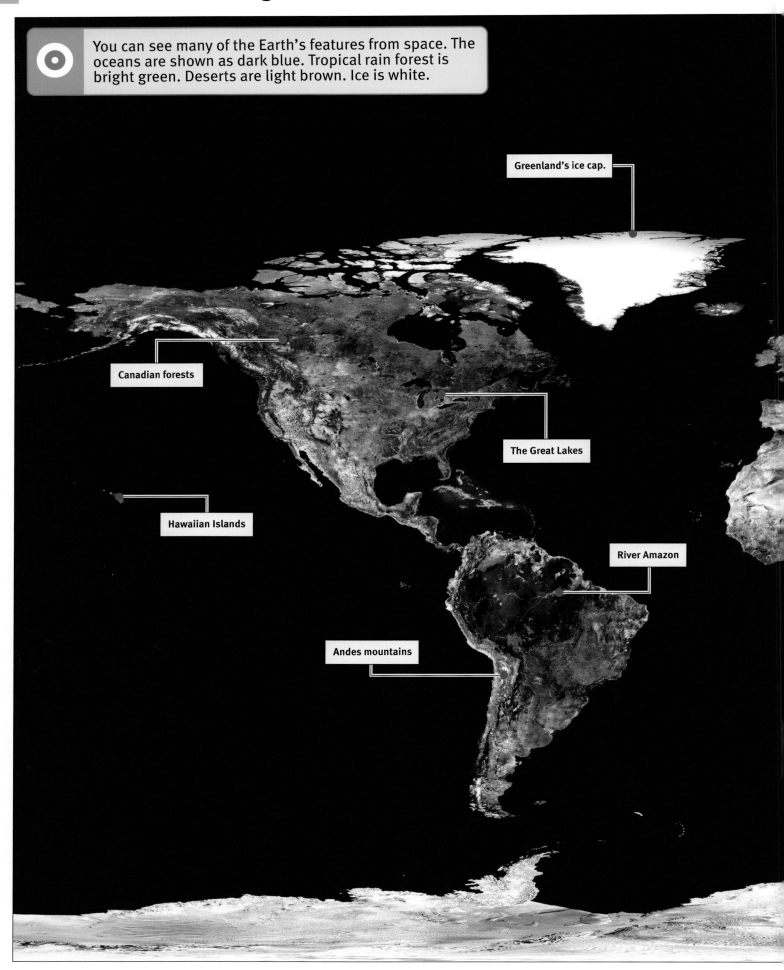

You can see many of the Earth's features from space. The oceans are shown as dark blue. Tropical rain forest is bright green. Deserts are light brown. Ice is white.

Greenland's ice cap.

Canadian forests

The Great Lakes

Hawaiian Islands

River Amazon

Andes mountains

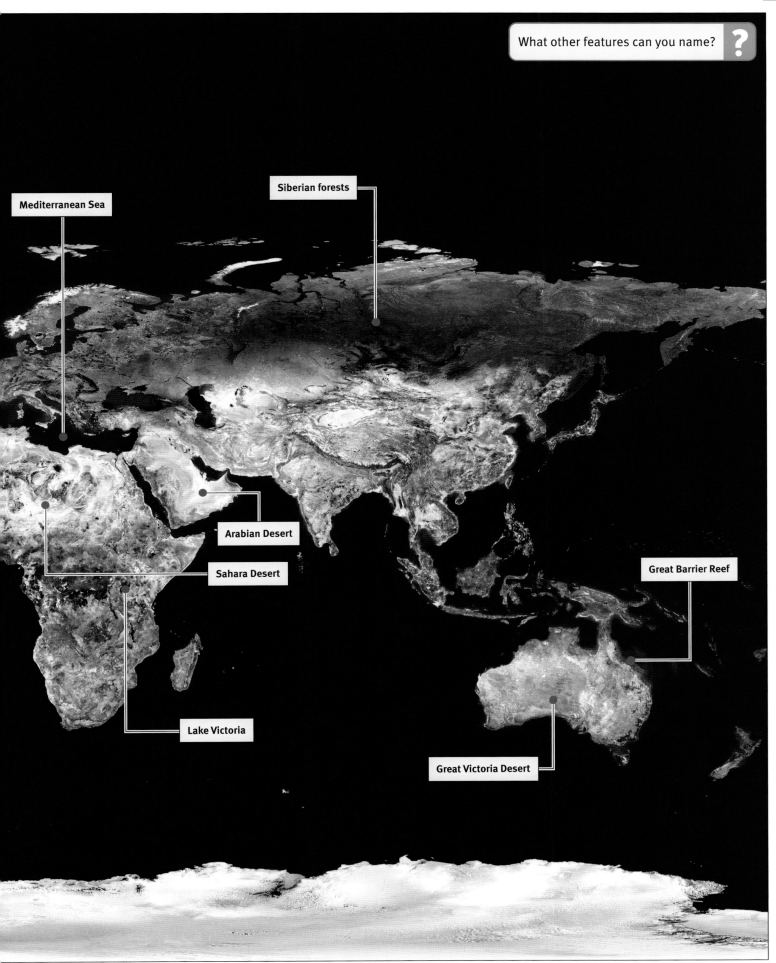

What other features can you name? **?**

Siberian forests

Mediterranean Sea

Arabian Desert

Sahara Desert

Great Barrier Reef

Lake Victoria

Great Victoria Desert

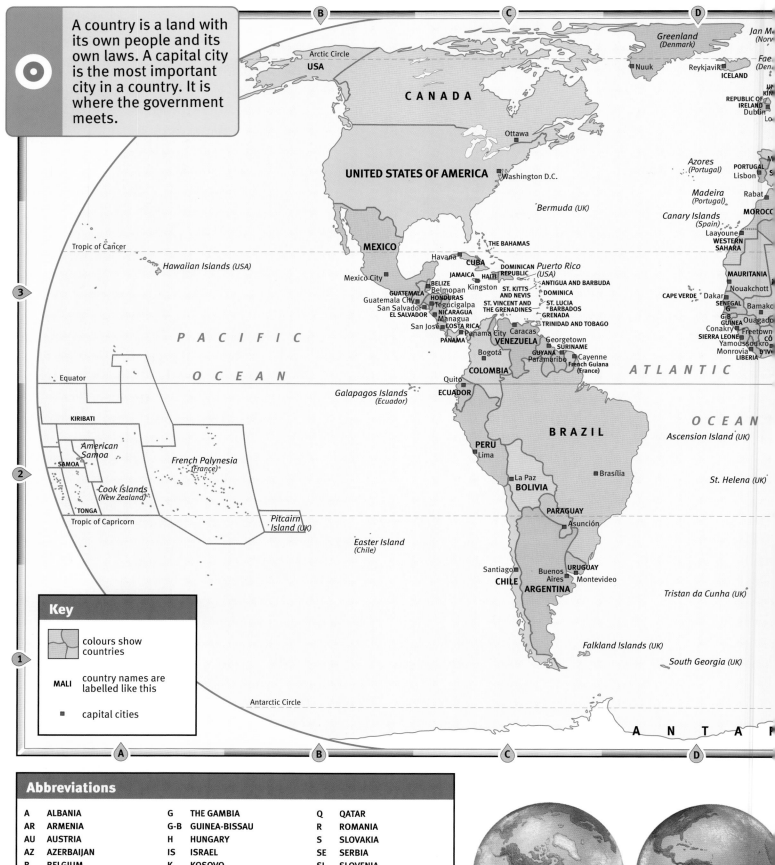

A country is a land with its own people and its own laws. A capital city is the most important city in a country. It is where the government meets.

Arctic Circle

USA

C A N A D A

Ottawa

UNITED STATES OF AMERICA

Washington D.C.

Tropic of Cancer

Hawaiian Islands (USA)

Bermuda (UK)

MEXICO

THE BAHAMAS

Havana

CUBA

Mexico City

DOMINICAN *Puerto Rico*
REPUBLIC *(USA)*

JAMAICA **HAITI**
Kingston

ANTIGUA AND BARBUDA

BELIZE
Belmopan

ST. KITTS
AND NEVIS

DOMINICA

GUATEMALA
Guatemala City
HONDURAS
Tegucigalpa
San Salvador
EL SALVADOR **NICARAGUA**
Managua

ST. VINCENT AND
THE GRENADINES

ST. LUCIA
BARBADOS
GRENADA

COSTA RICA
San José

TRINIDAD AND TOBAGO

Panama City Caracas
PANAMA **VENEZUELA**

Georgetown
GUYANA **SURINAME**
Bogotá Paramaribo Cayenne
COLOMBIA *French Guiana*
(France)

P A C I F I C

O C E A N

Equator

Galapagos Islands
(Ecuador)

Quito

ECUADOR

A T L A N T I C

KIRIBATI

American
Samoa

French Polynesia
(France)

O C E A N

SAMOA

B R A Z I L

Ascension Island (UK)

PERU
Lima

SAMOA

Cook Islands
(New Zealand)

La Paz Brasília

BOLIVIA

St. Helena (UK)

TONGA

Tropic of Capricorn

Pitcairn
Island (UK)

PARAGUAY

Asunción

Easter Island
(Chile)

Santiago Buenos **URUGUAY**
CHILE Aires Montevideo
ARGENTINA

Tristan da Cunha (UK)

Falkland Islands (UK)

South Georgia (UK)

Antarctic Circle

A N T A...

Key

colours show countries

MALI country names are labelled like this

■ capital cities

Greenland
(Denmark)

Jan Me...
(Norv...

Nuuk Reykjavík Fae...
(Den...
ICELAND

REPUBLIC OF
IRELAND
Dublin
Lo...

Azores
(Portugal) **PORTUGAL**
Lisbon S...

Madeira
(Portugal) Rabat

Canary Islands **MOROCC...**
(Spain)
Laayoune
WESTERN
SAHARA

MAURITANIA

Nouakchott

CAPE VERDE Dakar
SENEGAL Bamako
G-B Ouagado...
GUINEA
Conakry Freetown CÔ
SIERRA LEONE Yamoussoukro
Monrovia D'IV...
LIBERIA

Abbreviations

A	ALBANIA	G	THE GAMBIA	Q	QATAR		
AR	ARMENIA	G-B	GUINEA-BISSAU	R	ROMANIA		
AU	AUSTRIA	H	HUNGARY	S	SLOVAKIA		
AZ	AZERBAIJAN	IS	ISRAEL	SE	SERBIA		
B	BELGIUM	K	KOSOVO	SL	SLOVENIA		
BE	BENIN	L	LEBANON	SW	SWITZERLAND		
BH	BOSNIA-HERZEGOVINA	LI	LITHUANIA	T	TAJIKISTAN		
BR	BRUNEI	LU	LUXEMBOURG	TU	TURKMENISTAN		
BU	BURKINA	M	FORMER YUGOSLAV	U	UGANDA		
C	CROATIA		REPUBLIC OF MACEDONIA	UAE	UNITED ARAB EMIRATES		
CAR	CENTRAL AFRICAN REPUBLIC	MT	MONTENEGRO	ZIM	ZIMBABWE		
CZ	CZECH REPUBLIC	N	NETHERLANDS				

North America

South America

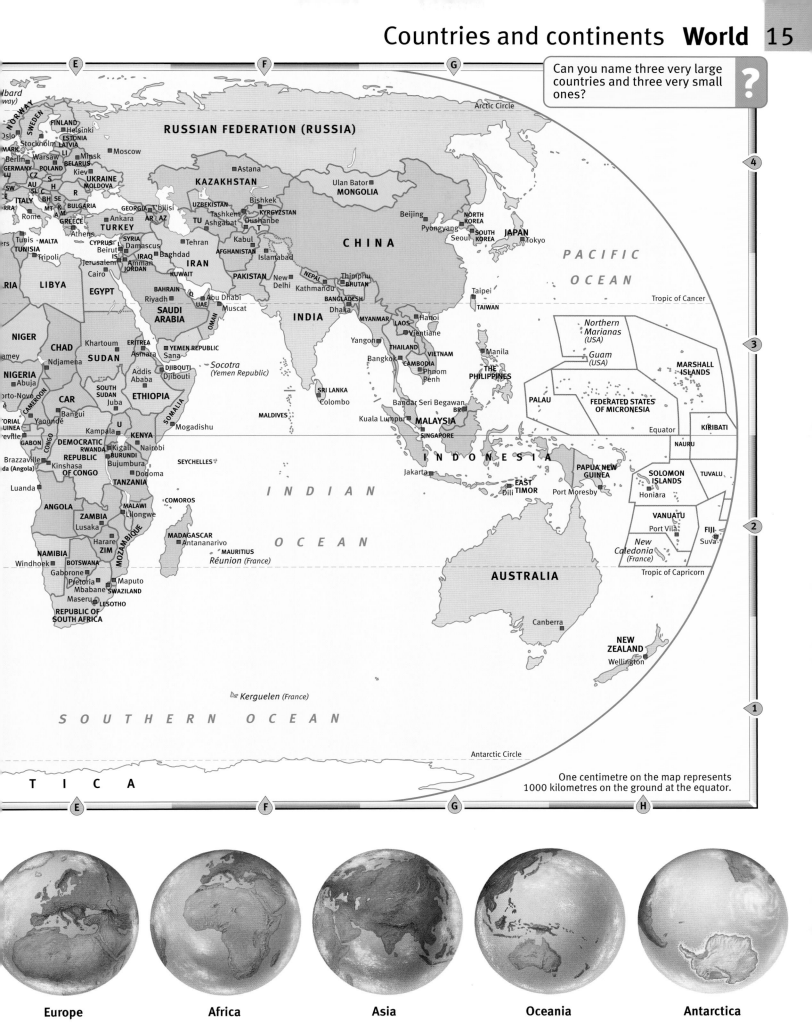

E · **F** · **G**

Arctic Circle

(lbard way)

NORWAY

SWEDEN

FINLAND

Helsinki

Oslo

Stockholm ESTONIA

MARK LATVIA

DENMARK LI

GERMANY Berlin Warsaw Minsk Moscow

BELARUS

LU POLAND

CZ S

AU R UKRAINE

SL K MOLDOVA

ITALY BH SE

MT K R

Rome BULGARIA

GREECE Ankara GEORGIA Tbilisi

MALTA TURKEY AR AZ

Athens

TUNISIA CYPRUS SYRIA Damascus

Tripoli Beirut IRAQ Baghdad

Jerusalem Amman

Cairo JORDAN

RUSSIAN FEDERATION (RUSSIA)

Astana

KAZAKHSTAN

Ulan Bator

MONGOLIA

Bishkek

UZBEKISTAN KYRGYZSTAN

Tashkent Beijing

Ashgabat Dushanbe

TU T

Tehran Kabul

IRAN AFGHANISTAN Islamabad CHINA

Pyongyang NORTH KOREA

Seoul SOUTH JAPAN

KOREA

Tokyo

PACIFIC

OCEAN

KUWAIT

LIBYA

EGYPT BAHRAIN Riyadh Q UAE Abu Dhabi

SAUDI Muscat

ARABIA OMAN

PAKISTAN New

Delhi NEPAL Thimphu

Kathmandu BHUTAN

BANGLADESH

INDIA Dhaka

MYANMAR LAOS Hanoi

Yangon Vientiane

THAILAND VIETNAM

Bangkok CAMBODIA

Phnom

Penh

Taipei

TAIWAN

Tropic of Cancer

Northern

Marianas

(USA)

Guam

(USA)

MARSHALL

ISLANDS

NIGER CHAD SUDAN Khartoum ERITREA Asmara

Ndjamena YEMEN REPUBLIC

Sana

NIGERIA Addis DJIBOUTI

Abuja SOUTH Ababa Djibouti Socotra (Yemen Republic)

orto-Novo CAMEROON SUDAN Juba ETHIOPIA

è Yaoundé CAR Bangui SRI LANKA

TORIAL U Colombo

UINEA Kampala

eville GABON DEMOCRATIC KENYA Mogadishu MALDIVES

Brazzaville CONGO RWANDA Kigali Nairobi

da (Angola) REPUBLIC BURUNDI SEYCHELLES

Kinshasa OF CONGO Bujumbura

Luanda Dodoma COMOROS

TANZANIA

ANGOLA

ZAMBIA MALAWI

Lusaka Lilongwe MADAGASCAR

Harare Antananarivo MAURITIUS

NAMIBIA ZIM Réunion (France)

Windhoek BOTSWANA

Gaborone Maputo

Pretoria Mbabane SWAZILAND

Maseru LESOTHO

REPUBLIC OF

SOUTH AFRICA

SOMALIA

THE PHILIPPINES

Manila

Bandar Seri Begawan

Kuala Lumpur BR

MALAYSIA

SINGAPORE

I N D O N E S I A

Jakarta PAPUA NEW

EAST GUINEA

TIMOR Port Moresby

Dili

PALAU

FEDERATED STATES

OF MICRONESIA

Equator

NAURU

SOLOMON

ISLANDS

Honiara

KIRIBATI

TUVALU

VANUATU

Port Vila FIJI

New Suva

Caledonia

(France)

I N D I A N

O C E A N

Tropic of Capricorn

AUSTRALIA

Canberra

Kerguelen (France)

S O U T H E R N   O C E A N

NEW

ZEALAND

Wellington

Antarctic Circle

One centimetre on the map represents

1000 kilometres on the ground at the equator.

T I C A

E · **F** · **G** · **H**

4

3

2

1

Europe

Africa

Asia

Oceania

Antarctica

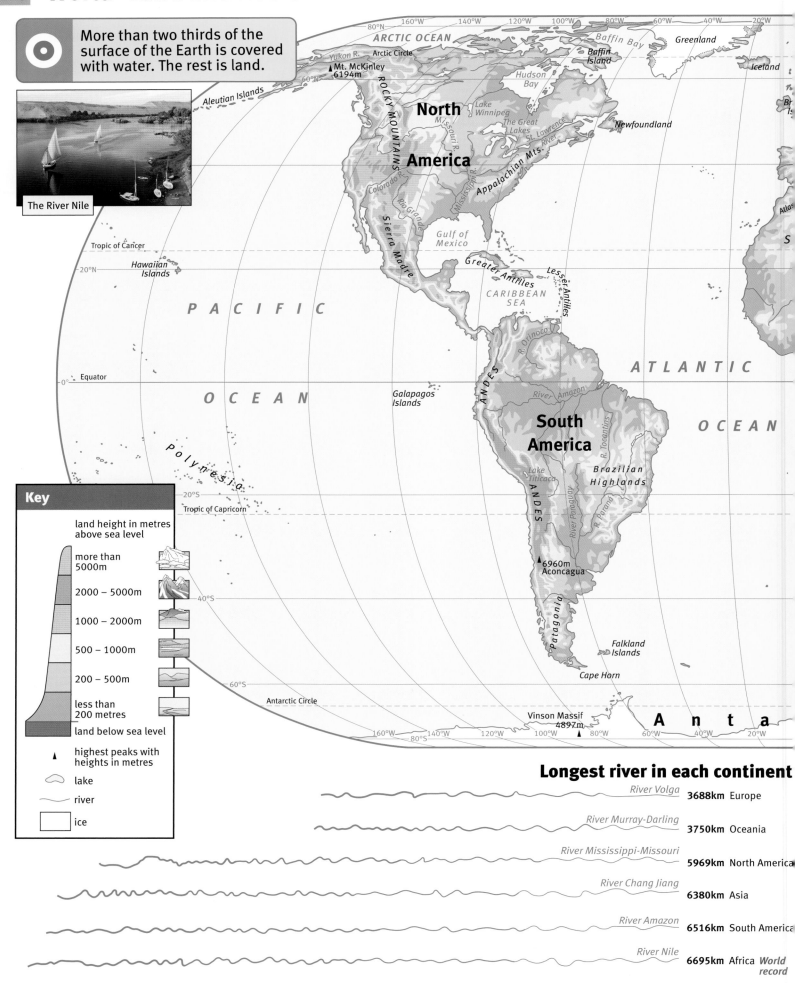

More than two thirds of the surface of the Earth is covered with water. The rest is land.

The River Nile

Key

land height in metres above sea level

more than 5000m

2000 – 5000m

1000 – 2000m

500 – 1000m

200 – 500m

less than 200 metres

land below sea level

▲ highest peaks with heights in metres

lake

river

ice

ARCTIC OCEAN

Arctic Circle

Yukon R.

▲ Mt. McKinley 6194m

Aleutian Islands

North America

ROCKY MOUNTAINS

Missouri R.

Colorado R.

Rio Grande

Sierra Madre

Mississippi R.

Appalachian Mts.

St. Lawrence River

The Great Lakes

Lake Winnipeg

Hudson Bay

Baffin Bay

Baffin Island

Greenland

Iceland

Newfoundland

Tropic of Cancer

20°N

Hawaiian Islands

PACIFIC

OCEAN

Equator

0°

Galapagos Islands

Gulf of Mexico

Greater Antilles

CARIBBEAN SEA

Lesser Antilles

R. Orinoco

River Amazon

ATLANTIC

OCEAN

South America

ANDES

Lake Titicaca

R. Tocantins

Brazilian Highlands

River Paraguay

R. Paraná

Polynesia

Tropic of Capricorn

20°S

▲ 6960m Aconcagua

ANDES

Patagonia

Falkland Islands

Cape Horn

40°S

60°S

Antarctic Circle

Vinson Massif 4897m ▲

Anta

Longest river in each continent

River Volga **3688km** Europe

River Murray-Darling **3750km** Oceania

River Mississippi-Missouri **5969km** North America

River Chang Jiang **6380km** Asia

River Amazon **6516km** South America

River Nile **6695km** Africa *World record*

© Oxford University Press
Eckert IV Projection

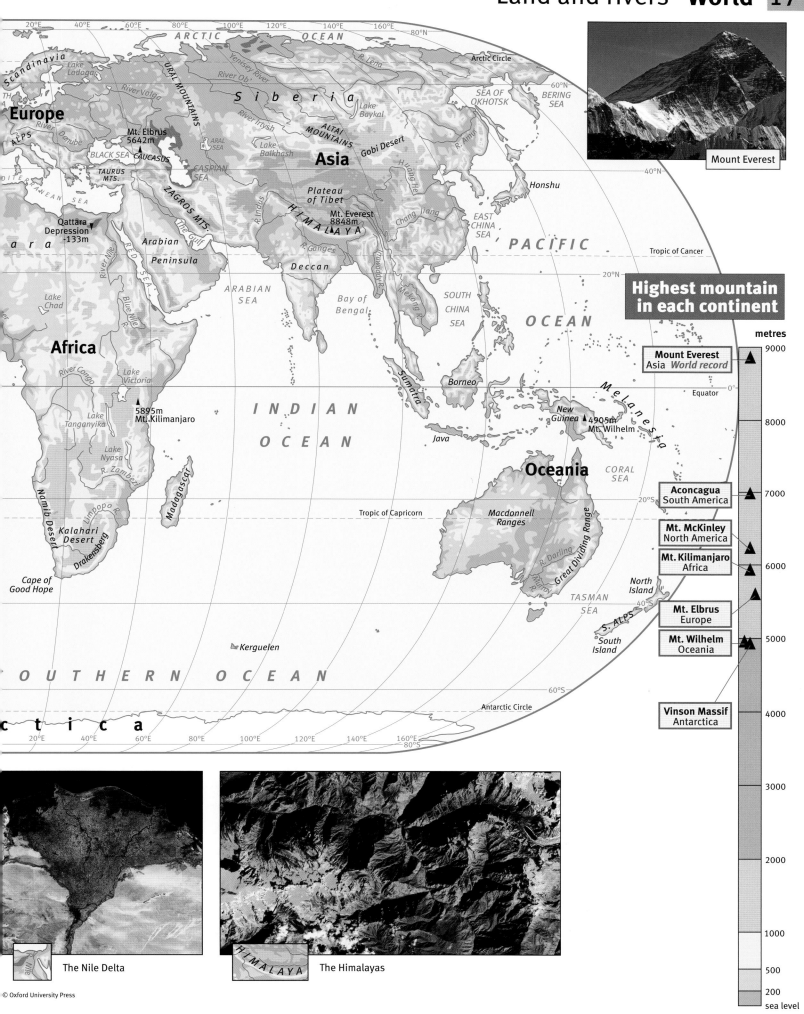

Mount Everest

Highest mountain in each continent

metres

Mount Everest
Asia *World record* ▲ 9000

Equator 0°

8000

Aconcagua
South America ▲ 7000

Mt. McKinley
North America ▲

Mt. Kilimanjaro
Africa ▲ 6000

Mt. Elbrus
Europe ▲

Mt. Wilhelm
Oceania ▲ 5000

Vinson Massif
Antarctica 4000

3000

2000

1000

500

200

sea level

Map labels

20°E 40°E 60°E 80°E 100°E 120°E 140°E 160°E 80°N

ARCTIC OCEAN

Arctic Circle

Scandinavia
Lake Ladoga
River Volga
URAL MOUNTAINS
Yenisey River
River Ob'
S i b e r i a
R. Lena
60°N
SEA OF OKHOTSK
BERING SEA

Europe
ALPS
River Danube
Mt. Elbrus 5642m
BLACK SEA CAUCASUS
TAURUS MTS.
ARAL SEA
River Irtysh
Lake Balkhash
ALTAI MOUNTAINS
Lake Baykal
Gobi Desert
R. Amur
Asia
Honshu
40°N

MEDITERRANEAN SEA
ZAGROS MTS
CASPIAN SEA
The Gulf
R. Indus
Plateau of Tibet
H I M A L A Y A
Mt. Everest 8848m ▲
Huang He
Chang Jiang
EAST CHINA SEA

Qattara Depression -133m
Sahara
Arabian Peninsula
RED SEA
River Nile
ARABIAN SEA
R. Ganges
Deccan
Irrawaddy R.
Bay of Bengal
Mekong R.
SOUTH CHINA SEA
PACIFIC
Tropic of Cancer

Lake Chad
Blue Nile R.
Africa
20°N

OCEAN
20°N

River Congo
Lake Victoria
5895m
Mt. Kilimanjaro ▲
Sumatra
Borneo
Java
New Guinea ▲ 4905m
Mt. Wilhelm
Melanesia

Lake Tanganyika
Lake Nyasa
R. Zambezi
I N D I A N   O C E A N

Namib Desert
Kalahari Desert
Limpopo R.
Madagascar
Drakensberg
Oceania
CORAL SEA

Cape of Good Hope
Tropic of Capricorn
Macdonnell Ranges
20°S

R. Darling
Great Dividing Range
North Island
R. Murray
TASMAN SEA
40°S
S. ALPS
South Island

Kerguelen

S O U T H E R N   O C E A N
60°S

Antarctic Circle

A n t a r c t i c a
20°E 40°E 60°E 80°E 100°E 120°E 140°E 160°E 80°S

The Nile Delta

HIMALAYA The Himalayas

© Oxford University Press

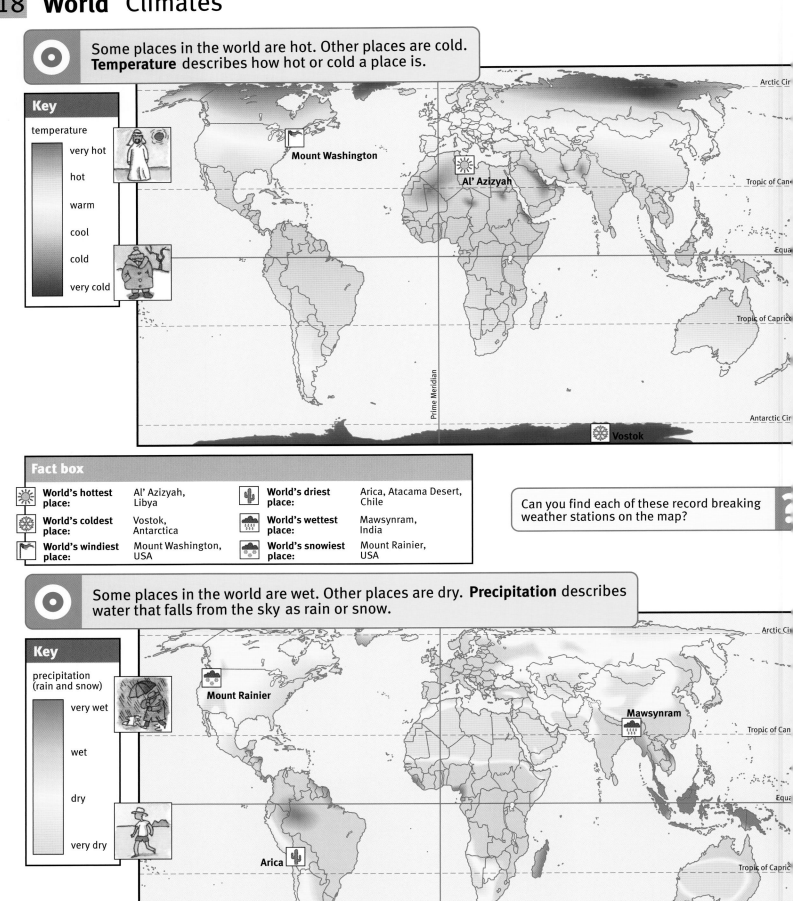

Some places in the world are hot. Other places are cold. **Temperature** describes how hot or cold a place is.

Key

temperature

- very hot
- hot
- warm
- cool
- cold
- very cold

Mount Washington

Al' Azizyah

Vostok

Fact box

World's hottest place:	Al' Azizyah, Libya	
World's coldest place:	Vostok, Antarctica	
World's windiest place:	Mount Washington, USA	

World's driest place:	Arica, Atacama Desert, Chile
World's wettest place:	Mawsynram, India
World's snowiest place:	Mount Rainier, USA

Can you find each of these record breaking weather stations on the map?

Some places in the world are wet. Other places are dry. **Precipitation** describes water that falls from the sky as rain or snow.

Key

precipitation (rain and snow)

- very wet
- wet
- dry
- very dry

Mount Rainier

Mawsynram

Arica

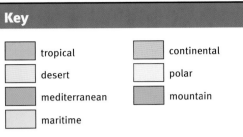

Patterns of temperature and precipitation throughout the year create different types of climate.

Key

tropical	continental
desert	polar
mediterranean	mountain
maritime	

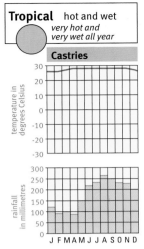

Tropical hot and wet
very hot and very wet all year

Castries

temperature in degrees Celsius

rainfall in millimetres

J F M A M J J A S O N D

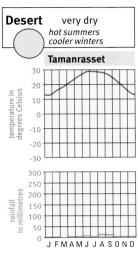

Desert very dry
hot summers cooler winters

Tamanrasset

temperature in degrees Celsius

rainfall in millimetres

J F M A M J J A S O N D

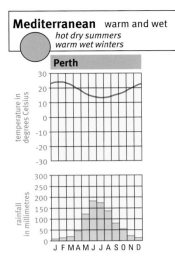

Mediterranean warm and wet
hot dry summers warm wet winters

Perth

temperature in degrees Celsius

rainfall in millimetres

J F M A M J J A S O N D

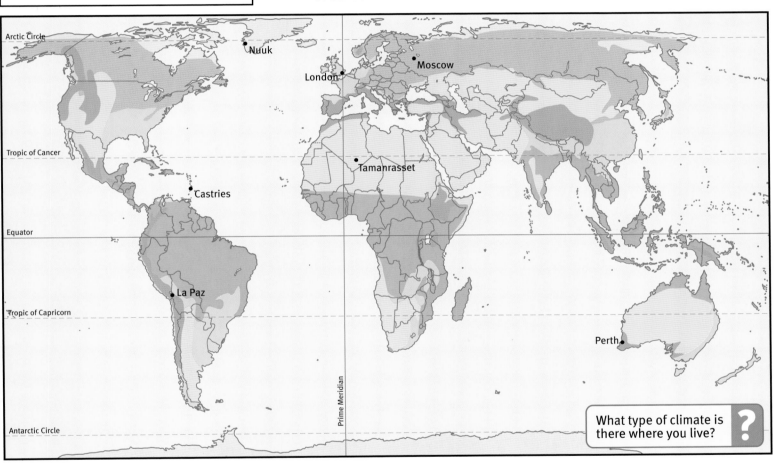

Arctic Circle

Nuuk

Moscow

London

Tropic of Cancer

Tamanrasset

Castries

Equator

La Paz

Tropic of Capricorn

Perth

Prime Meridian

Antarctic Circle

What type of climate is there where you live? **?**

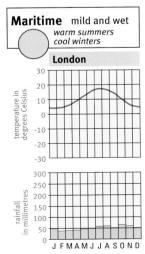

Maritime mild and wet
warm summers cool winters

London

temperature in degrees Celsius

rainfall in millimetres

J F M A M J J A S O N D

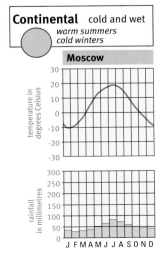

Continental cold and wet
warm summers cold winters

Moscow

temperature in degrees Celsius

rainfall in millimetres

J F M A M J J A S O N D

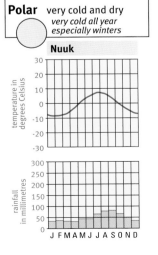

Polar very cold and dry
very cold all year especially winters

Nuuk

temperature in degrees Celsius

rainfall in millimetres

J F M A M J J A S O N D

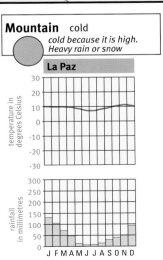

Mountain cold
cold because it is high. Heavy rain or snow

La Paz

temperature in degrees Celsius

rainfall in millimetres

J F M A M J J A S O N D

Each of the major world environments shown on the map has its own special climate, plant life and animals. Most natural environments have been influenced by people.

deciduous forest

coniferous forest

tropical forest

Key

	coniferous forest	trees have leaves all year
	deciduous forest	trees drop their leaves in winter
	tropical forest	tall trees growing close together
	savannah	tall grass and scattered trees
	temperate grassland	prairies, steppes, pampas and veld
	semi desert	short grass and small dry bushes
	desert	sand and stones with few plants
	tundra	moss and bog with some short trees
	ice	no plants
	mountains	thin soils and steep slopes

ARCTIC OCEAN

Arctic Circle

PACIFIC OCEAN

ATLANTIC OCEAN

Tropic of Cancer

Equator

Tropic of Capricorn

Antarctic Circle

desert

semi desert

What type of environment is most common along the equator? **?**

savannah

temperate grassland

ARCTIC OCEAN

Arctic Circle

60°N

40°N

PACIFIC

Tropic of Cancer

20°N

OCEAN

INDIAN

OCEAN

Equator 0°

SOUTHERN OCEAN

20°S

Tropic of Capricorn

40°S

© Oxford University Press

60°S

Antarctic Circle

20°E 40°E 60°E 80°E 100°E 120°E 140°E 160°E 80°N

20°E 40°E 60°E 80°E 100°E 120°E 140°E 160°E 80°S

tundra

mountains

ice

People have damaged the environment in many parts of the world. Cutting down forests and burning fossil fuels affects the Earth's atmosphere and can cause **climate change**.

Key

🌳	tropical rain forest
	areas where rain forest has been cut down
	desert
	areas that are becoming desert
	areas most affected by air pollution
	sea areas most affected by oil pollution
	areas where ice is melting

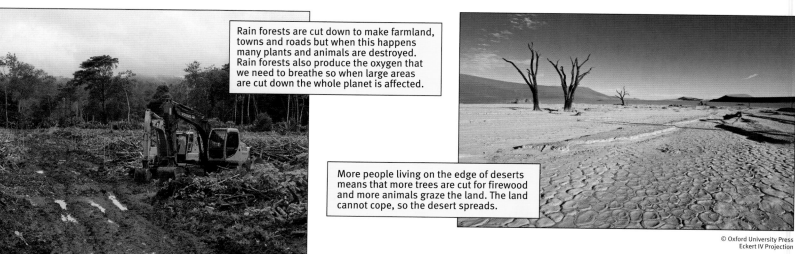

Rain forests are cut down to make farmland, towns and roads but when this happens many plants and animals are destroyed. Rain forests also produce the oxygen that we need to breathe so when large areas are cut down the whole planet is affected.

More people living on the edge of deserts means that more trees are cut for firewood and more animals graze the land. The land cannot cope, so the desert spreads.

Sustainability means looking after the Earth's land, air and water so that they last for everyone in the future.

ARCTIC OCEAN

Arctic Circle

BLACK SEA

MEDITERRANEAN SEA

ARABIAN SEA

EAST CHINA SEA

PACIFIC OCEAN

Tropic of Cancer

SOUTH CHINA SEA

Equator

INDIAN OCEAN

Tropic of Capricorn

SOUTHERN OCEAN

Antarctic Circle

The world's great ice sheets are melting as the world's climate becomes warmer.

Motor vehicles and burning fossil fuels are the greatest cause of air pollution.

Oil spilt from ships and oil rigs can damage beaches and wildlife. Birds with oil on their wings cannot fly.

© Oxford University Press

There are about 6 500 000 000 people in the world. They are spread very unevenly. Some places are very crowded. Other places have very few people.

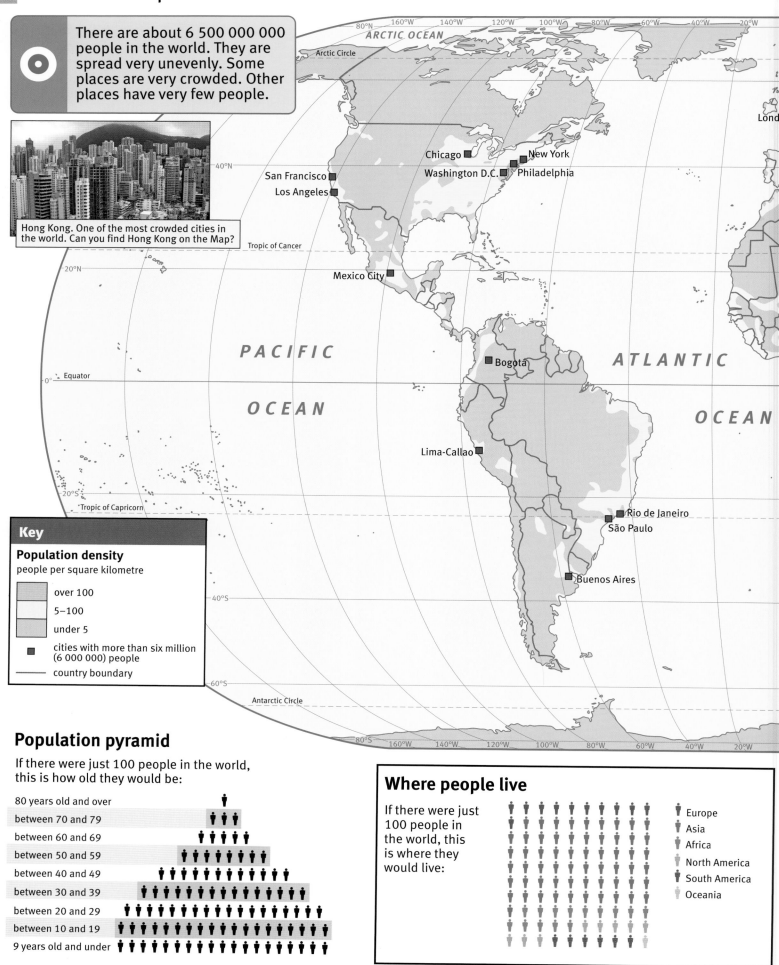

Hong Kong. One of the most crowded cities in the world. Can you find Hong Kong on the Map?

Key

Population density

people per square kilometre

	over 100
	5–100
	under 5
■	cities with more than six million (6 000 000) people
—	country boundary

Population pyramid

If there were just 100 people in the world, this is how old they would be:

80 years old and over	
between 70 and 79	
between 60 and 69	
between 50 and 59	
between 40 and 49	
between 30 and 39	
between 20 and 29	
between 10 and 19	
9 years old and under	

Where people live

If there were just 100 people in the world, this is where they would live:

- Europe
- Asia
- Africa
- North America
- South America
- Oceania

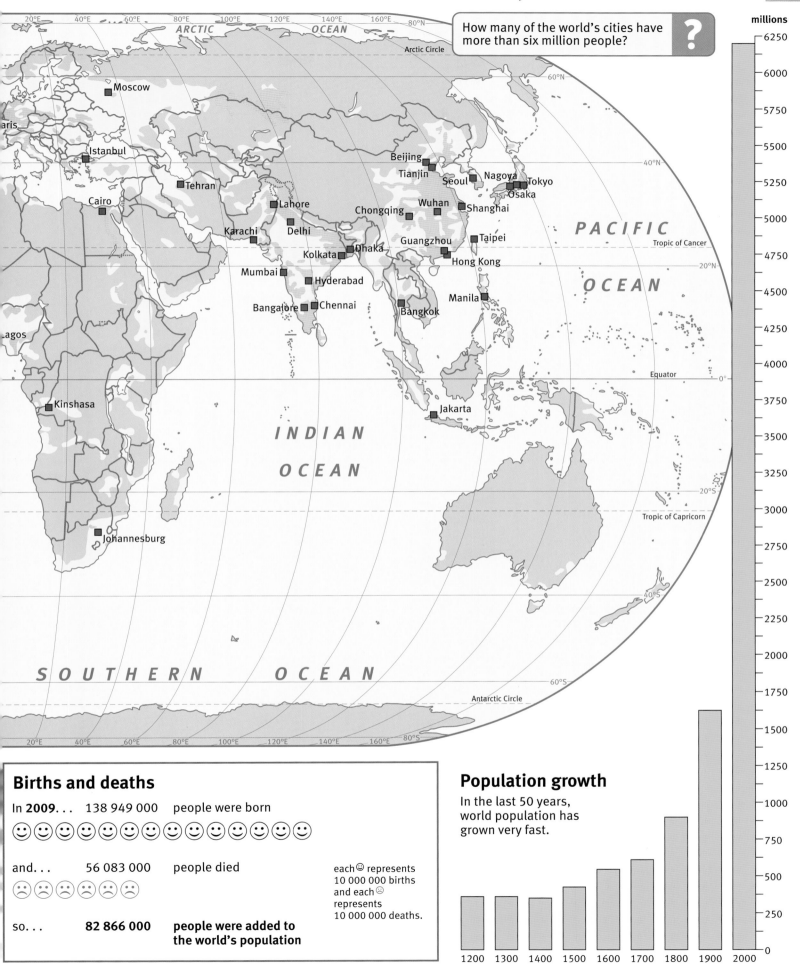

ARCTIC   OCEAN

Arctic Circle

60°N

Paris

Moscow

Istanbul

Beijing
40°N
Tianjin   Seoul   Nagoya
Tehran   Tokyo
Osaka
Cairo   Lahore   Wuhan
Chongqing   Shanghai
Karachi   Delhi   PACIFIC
Dhaka   Guangzhou   Taipei
Kolkata   Tropic of Cancer
Mumbai   Hyderabad   Hong Kong
20°N
Bangalore   Chennai   OCEAN
Lagos   Manila
Bangkok

Equator   0°

Kinshasa

Jakarta

INDIAN

OCEAN

20°S

Johannesburg

Tropic of Capricorn

40°S

SOUTHERN   OCEAN

60°S

Antarctic Circle

20°E 40°E 60°E 80°E 100°E 120°E 140°E 160°E 80°S

How many of the world's cities have more than six million people? ?

millions

6250
6000
5750
5500
5250
5000
4750
4500
4250
4000
3750
3500
3250
3000
2750
2500
2250
2000
1750
1500
1250
1000
750
500
250
0

Births and deaths

In **2009**... 138 949 000 people were born

☺ ☺ ☺ ☺ ☺ ☺ ☺ ☺ ☺ ☺ ☺ ☺ ☺ ☺

and... 56 083 000 people died

☹ ☹ ☹ ☹ ☹

so... **82 866 000** **people were added to the world's population**

each ☺ represents 10 000 000 births and each ☹ represents 10 000 000 deaths.

Population growth

In the last 50 years, world population has grown very fast.

1200 1300 1400 1500 1600 1700 1800 1900 2000

Travel and communication around the world are becoming faster but some places are better connected than others.

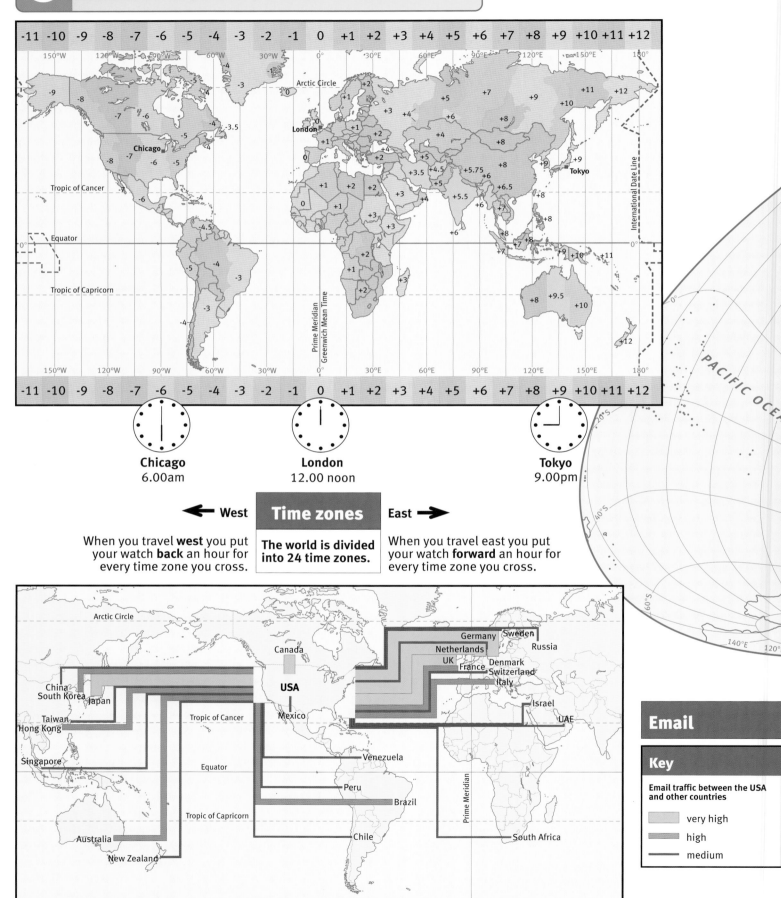

Chicago
6.00am

London
12.00 noon

Tokyo
9.00pm

← West **Time zones** East →

When you travel **west** you put your watch **back** an hour for every time zone you cross.

The world is divided into 24 time zones.

When you travel east you put your watch **forward** an hour for every time zone you cross.

Email

Key

Email traffic between the USA and other countries

- very high
- high
- medium

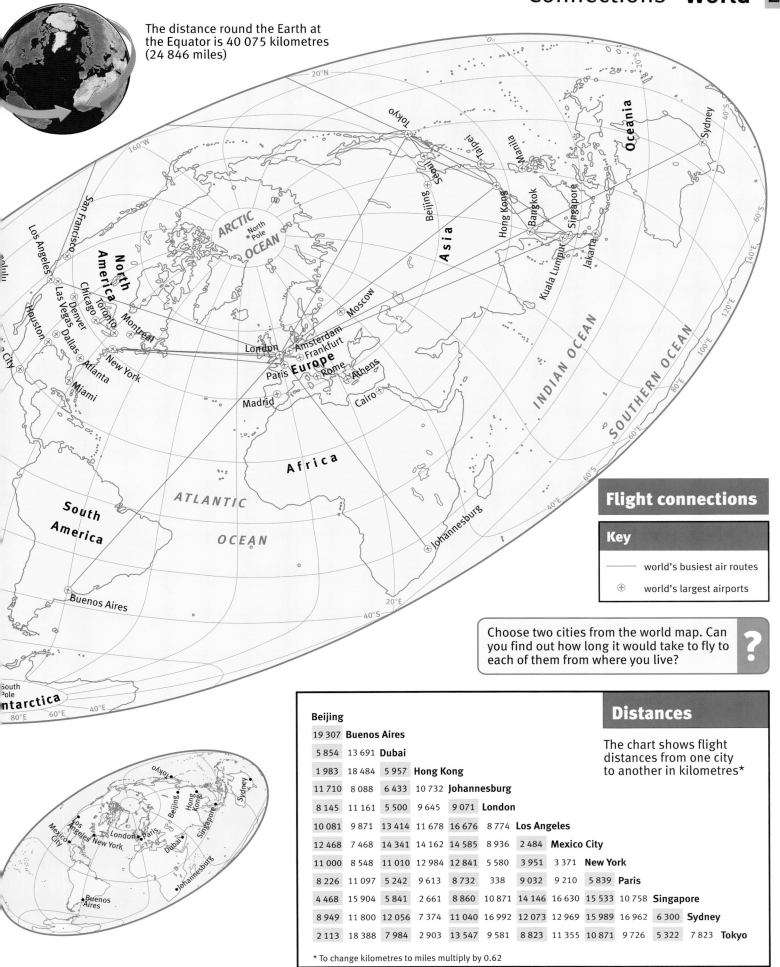

The distance round the Earth at the Equator is 40 075 kilometres (24 846 miles)

Flight connections

Key

—— world's busiest air routes

⊕ world's largest airports

Choose two cities from the world map. Can you find out how long it would take to fly to each of them from where you live? **?**

Distances

The chart shows flight distances from one city to another in kilometres*

Beijing											
19 307	**Buenos Aires**										
5 854	13 691	**Dubai**									
1 983	18 484	5 957	**Hong Kong**								
11 710	8 088	6 433	10 732	**Johannesburg**							
8 145	11 161	5 500	9 645	9 071	**London**						
10 081	9 871	13 414	11 678	16 676	8 774	**Los Angeles**					
12 468	7 468	14 341	14 162	14 585	8 936	2 484	**Mexico City**				
11 000	8 548	11 010	12 984	12 841	5 580	3 951	3 371	**New York**			
8 226	11 097	5 242	9 613	8 732	338	9 032	9 210	5 839	**Paris**		
4 468	15 904	5 841	2 661	8 860	10 871	14 146	16 630	15 533	10 758	**Singapore**	
8 949	11 800	12 056	7 374	11 040	16 992	12 073	12 969	15 989	16 962	6 300	**Sydney**
2 113	18 388	7 984	2 903	13 547	9 581	8 823	11 355	10 871	9 726	5 322	7 823	**Tokyo**

* To change kilometres to miles multiply by 0.62

Oblique Aitoff Projection

Europe is a continent of peninsulas and islands. The Ural Mountains form its eastern boundary.

A B C D E F

20°E 40°E 60°E

3

GREENLAND SEA

20°W

Iceland
▲1491m
Mount
Hekla

N

Lofoten
Islands

Kola
Peninsula

Lappland

WHITE
SEA

River North Dvina

URAL MOUNTAINS

River Ob

River Pechora

60°N

ATLANTIC
OCEAN

20°W

Faroe
Islands

Shetland
Islands

Orkney
Islands

NORTH
SEA

S c a n d i n a v i a

Gulf of Bothnia

Lake
Vänern

Gotland

Lake
Onega

Lake
Ladoga

Lake
Peipus

Rybinsk
Reservoir

River Volga

2

Ireland

Great
Britain

BALTIC SEA

Lake
Vättern

C e n t r a l
R u s s i a n
U p l a n d s

English Channel

R. Thames

Friesian Islands

River Elbe

Bornholm

North European Plain

River Oder

River Vistula

River Dnieper

River Don

River Donets

Bay of
Biscay

R. Rhine

River Seine

River Loire

Cape
Finisterre

Cantabrian Mts.

Pyrénées

River Duero

River Ebro

R. Tagus

Massif
Central

R. Rhône

Jura

4807m▲
Mont Blanc

A L P S

River Po

CARPATHIANS

R. Dniester

Hungarian
Basin

2548m▲

River Danube

SEA OF
AZOV

BLACK   SEA

CASPIAN
SEA

C A U C A S U S

5642m▲
Mt. Elbrus

Corsica

APPENNINES

Dinaric Alps

ADRIATIC
SEA

Pindus Mountains

AEGEAN SEA

Anatolian
Plateau

5123m▲
Mt. Ararat

Lake
Van

40°

Cape
St. Vincent

Balearic Islands

Menorca

Mallorca

Ibiza

Sardinia

TYRRHENIAN
SEA

Mt. Etna
3323m▲

Sicily

M E D I T E R R A N E A N

IONIAN
SEA

2917m▲
Mt. Olympus

Peloponnese

Malta

S E A

Crete

Rhodes

Cyprus

Taurus Mountains

20°E

40°E

1

Key

land height in metres
above sea level

more than
2000m

1000 – 2000m

500 – 1000m

200 – 500m

less than
200 metres

land below sea level

▲ highest peaks with
heights in metres

⌒ lake

～ river

Fact box

	area:	10 214 392km²
▲	**highest point:**	Mt. Elbrus 5 642m
▼	**lowest point:**	Caspian Sea 28m below sea level
〰	**longest river:**	River Volga 3 688km

Scale

One centimetre on the map
represents 240 kilometres
on the ground.

0   240   480   720km

Can you name the mountains
that lie between Spain and
France?

?

C D

A B C D E F

3

2

1

Europeans have settled all over the world and European languages can be heard in every other continent.

20°W 0° 20°E 40°E 60°E

Arctic Circle

ICELAND
Reykjavik

N

ATLANTIC OCEAN

60°N

NORWAY
SWEDEN
FINLAND

RUSSIAN FEDERATION (RUSSIA)

Oslo
Stockholm
Helsinki
St. Petersburg
Nizhniy-Novgorod

Göteborg
Tallinn
ESTONIA
Moscow

NORTH SEA

LATVIA
Riga

Belfast
Edinburgh
REPUBLIC OF IRELAND
Dublin
UNITED KINGDOM
Manchester
Birmingham

DENMARK
Copenhagen
BALTIC SEA
LITHUANIA
KALININGRAD (Russia)
Vilnius
Minsk
BELARUS

NETHERLANDS
Amsterdam
Hamburg
POLAND
Warsaw
Kharkov
Volgograd

London
Rotterdam
GERMANY
Berlin
BELGIUM
Düsseldorf
Brussels
LUXEMBOURG
Luxembourg
Prague
CZECH REP.
Krakow
UKRAINE
Donets'k
Rostov-on-Don

Paris
FRANCE
Munich
SLOVAKIA
Kiev

Bern
Vienna
Bratislava
MOLDOVA
SWITZERLAND
LIECHTENSTEIN
AUSTRIA
Budapest
Chisinau
Odessa

Bordeaux
Lyons
Milan
Ljubljana
SLOVENIA
HUNGARY
ROMANIA
Bucharest

Oporto
PORTUGAL
SPAIN
ANDORRA
Marseilles
MONACO
Zagreb
CROATIA
SAN MARINO
ITALY
BOSNIA–HERZEGOVINA
Sarajevo
Belgrade
SERBIA
Pristina
KOSOVO
BULGARIA
Sofia
BLACK SEA
GEORGIA
T'bilisi

Lisbon
Madrid
Barcelona
Rome
Podgorica
MONTENEGRO
Skopje
FYRO MACEDONIA
Istanbul
Ankara
Adana

Seville
Valencia
Naples
Tiranë
ALBANIA
GREECE
TURKEY
Izmir

Gibraltar (UK)
Ceuta (Sp.)
Melilla (Sp.)

MEDITERRANEAN SEA
Athens
Nicosia
CYPRUS
SYRIA

MOROCCO
ALGERIA
TUNISIA
Valletta
MALTA
LEBANON
IRAQ
ISRAEL
JORDAN

LIBYA
EGYPT
SAUDI ARABIA

Tropic of Cancer

Key

colours show countries

ITALY country names are labelled like this

capital cities

other important cities

Fact box

population: 655 884 785 people *
largest country: Ukraine 603 698km²
country with most people: Germany 82 698 000
largest city: Istanbul, Turkey 9 946 000

* does not include Russian Federation

Many languages are spoken in Europe How many can you name? ?

© Oxford University Press

The European Union (EU) was set up in 1957 so that its people could live in peace and have a better quality of life. Since then it has grown from six member countries to twenty-seven. Other countries hope to join.

The flag of the European Union

Key

	original member countries in 1957
	countries that joined 1973–1995
	countries that joined 2004–2007
	countries that have applied to join
⊙	countries that use the euro

Scale

One centimetre on the map represents 29 kilometres on the ground.

0   290   580   870

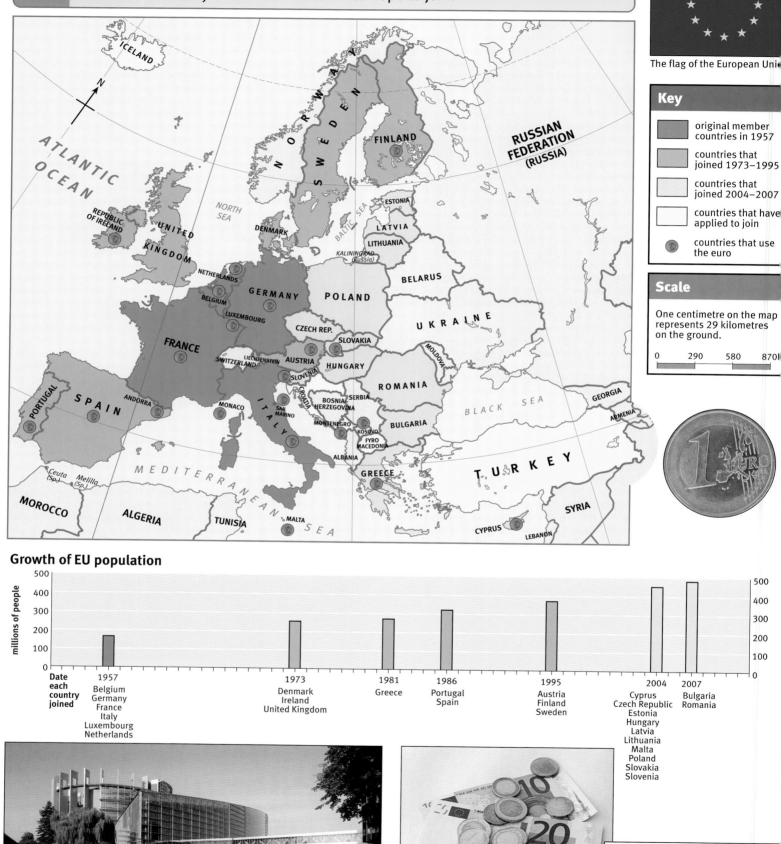

Growth of EU population

millions of people

Date each country joined	1957	1973	1981	1986	1995	2004	2007
	Belgium Germany France Italy Luxembourg Netherlands	Denmark Ireland United Kingdom	Greece	Portugal Spain	Austria Finland Sweden	Cyprus Czech Republic Estonia Hungary Latvia Lithuania Malta Poland Slovakia Slovenia	Bulgaria Romania

Laws that affect people living in EU countries are made by the European parliament which meets in this building in Strasbourg. The parliament also meets at the EU headquarters in Brussels.

Euro coins and notes were introduced in 2002 but not all European countries have agreed to use the Euro.

England, Scotland and Wales, together with Northern Ireland make the **United Kingdom**.

Hadrian's Wall was built across northern England nearly two thousand years ago. It was one of the frontiers of the Roman Empire.

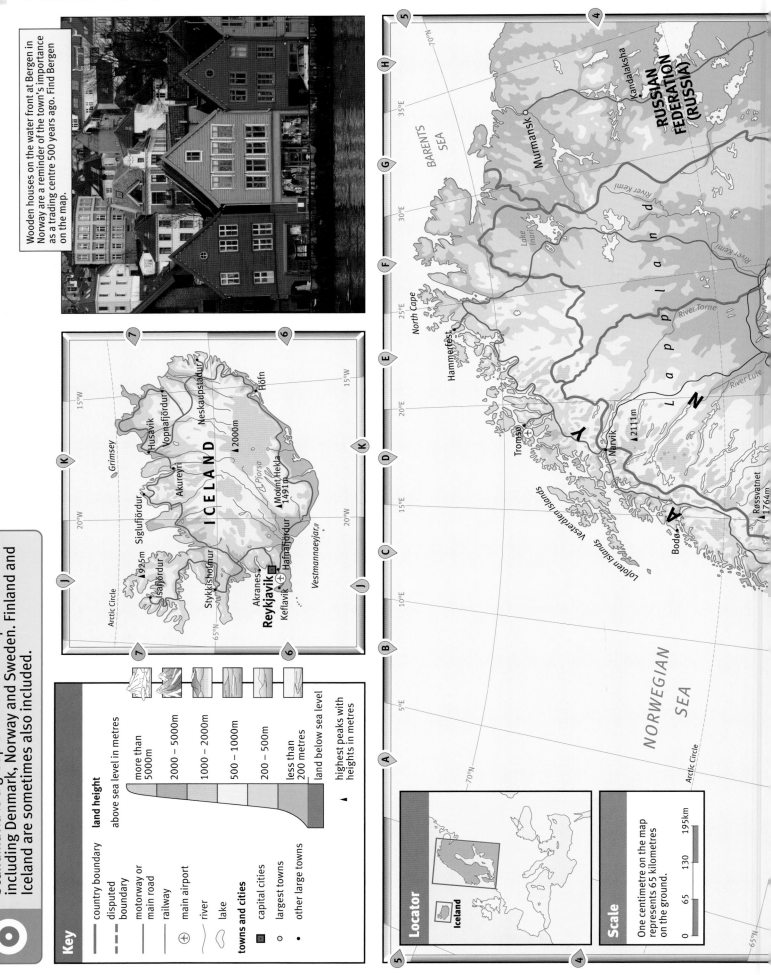

Wooden houses on the water front at Bergen in Norway are a reminder of the town's importance as a trading centre 500 years ago. Find Bergen on the map.

Scandinavia is a group of northern European countries including Denmark, Norway and Sweden. Finland and Iceland are sometimes also included.

Key

land height
above sea level in metres

	more than 5000m
	2000 – 5000m
	1000 – 2000m
	500 – 1000m
	200 – 500m
	less than 200 metres
	land below sea level

▲ highest peaks with heights in metres

country boundary
disputed boundary
motorway or main road
railway
⊕ main airport
river
lake

towns and cities
■ capital cities
○ largest towns
• other large towns

Locator

Iceland

Scale

One centimetre on the map represents 65 kilometres on the ground.

0   65   130   195km

ICELAND

Grimsey

Arctic Circle

Siglufjörður
▲935m
Ísafjörður
Husavík
Vopnafjörður
Akureyri
Neskaupstaður
▲2000m
Höfn
Stykkishólmur
Þjórsá
Mount Hekla ▲1491m
Akranes
Reykjavik
Keflavík ⊕ Hafnarfjörður
Vestmannaeyjar

20°W   15°W
65°N

RUSSIAN FEDERATION (RUSSIA)

BARENTS SEA

Kandalaksha
Murmansk

Lapland

Lake Inari
River Kemi

River Torne

River Lule

North Cape
Hammerfest

Tromsø ⊕
Narvik ▲2111m

Vesterålen Islands
Lofoten Islands
Bodø
Rossvatn ▲1764m

NORWEGIAN SEA

Arctic Circle
70°N
65°N

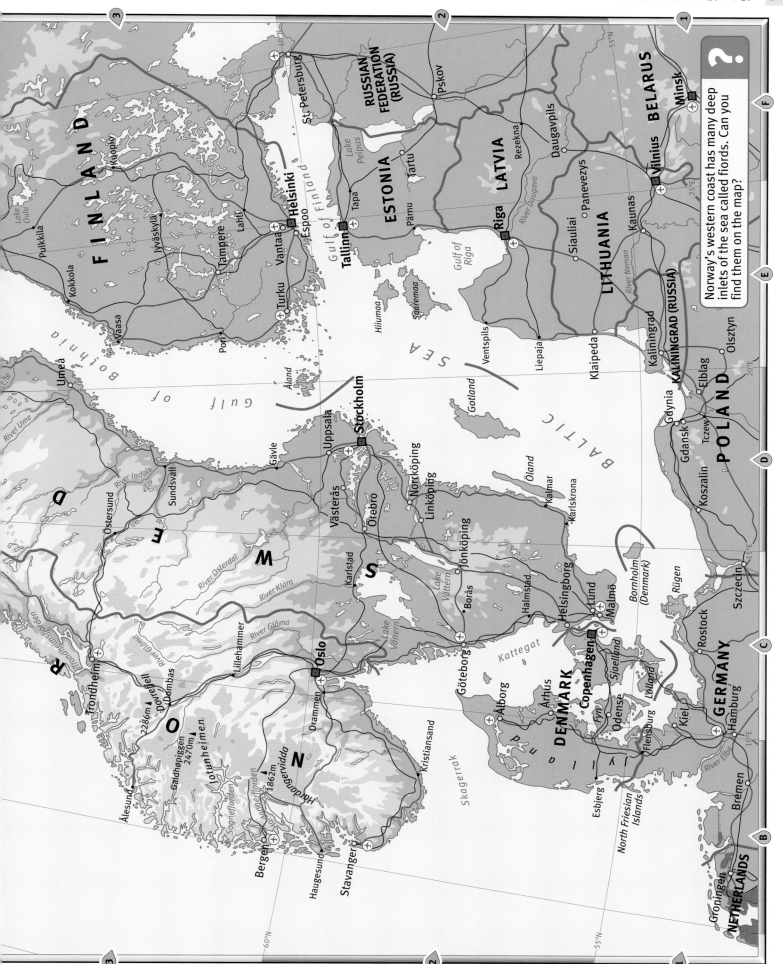

RUSSIAN FEDERATION (RUSSIA)

St. Petersburg
Pskov

FINLAND

Kuopio
Pulkkila
Kokkola
Jyväskylä
Tampere
Lahti
Vaasa
Turku
Pori
Vantaa
Espoo
Helsinki

Lake Oulu

Gulf of Finland

Tartu
Tapa
Pärnu

ESTONIA

Tallinn

Hiiumaa
Saaremaa

Lake Peipus

LATVIA

Riga
Rezekna
Daugavpils
River Daugava

Gulf of Riga

LITHUANIA

Siauliai
Panevezys
Kaunas
River Neman

BELARUS

Minsk
Vilnius

KALININGRAD (RUSSIA)
Kaliningrad

Ventspils
Liepaja
Klaipeda

25°E

Gotland
Öland

BALTIC SEA

POLAND

Gdynia
Gdansk
Tczew
Elblag
Olsztyn
Koszalin
Szczecin

20°E

Bornholm (Denmark)
Rügen

GERMANY

Rostock
Kiel
Hamburg
Bremen
River Elbe

10°E

Flensburg

North Friesian Islands
Esbjerg

NETHERLANDS
Groningen

Gulf of Bothnia

River Ume
Umeå
River Indals
Sundsvall
Östersund
River Österdal
River Klara
Gävle
Uppsala
Stockholm
Västerås
Örebro
Norrköping
Linköping
Lake Vättern
Jönköping
Borås
Karlstad
Lake Vänern

Åland

S W E D E N

Kalmar
Karlskrona
Halmstad
Helsingborg
Lund
Malmö
Göteborg
Helsingör

Kattegat

DENMARK

Ålborg
Århus
Odense
Fyn
Sjaelland
Lolland
Copenhagen

Skagerrak

Trondheim
Trondheimsfjorden
Ålesund
2286m
Dovrefjell
Dombas
Galdhöpiggen 2470m
Jotunheimen
1862m
Hardangervidda
Sognefjorden
Bergen
Haugesund
Stavanger
Kristiansand

N O R W A Y

Lillehammer
Drammen
Oslo
River Glåma

55°N
55°N
60°N

© Oxford University Press

> Norway's western coast has many deep inlets of the sea called fiords. Can you find them on the map?

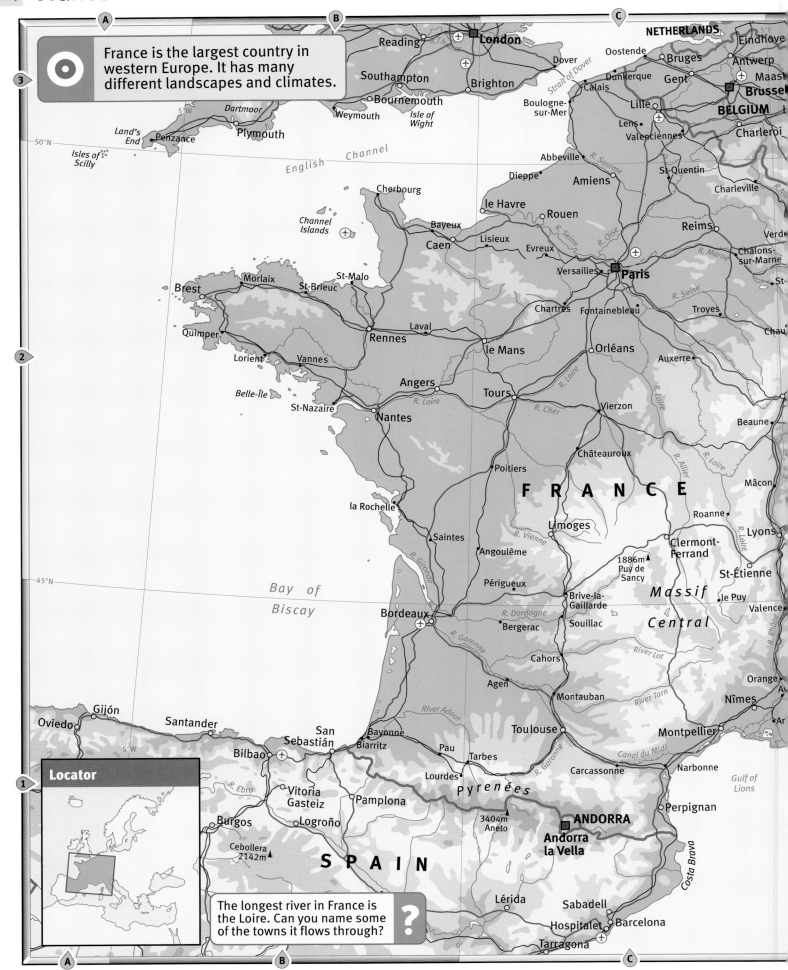

France is the largest country in western Europe. It has many different landscapes and climates.

The longest river in France is the Loire. Can you name some of the towns it flows through?

Locator

NETHERLANDS

BELGIUM

SPAIN

ANDORRA

F R A N C E

Massif Central

Bay of Biscay

English Channel

Pyrénées

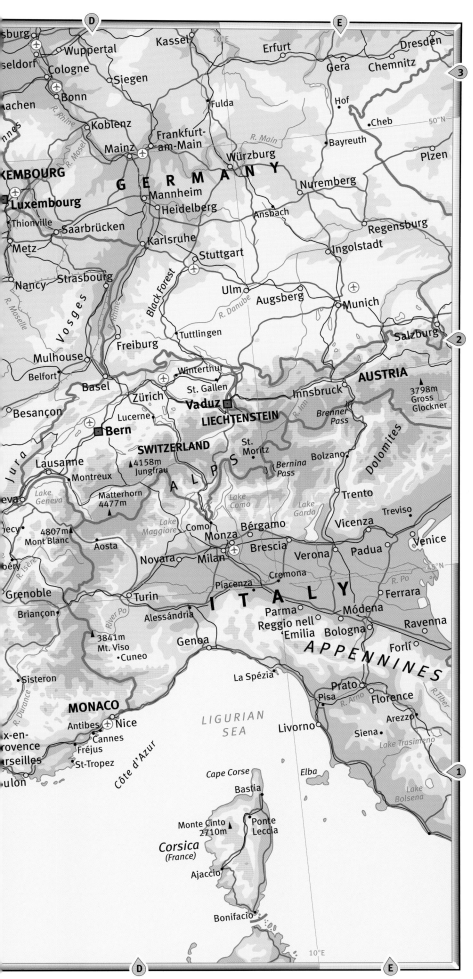

Key

——	country boundary
- - -	disputed boundary
——	motorway or main road
——	railway
✈	main airport
~~	river
◠	lake

towns and cities

■	capital cities
○	largest towns
•	other large towns

land height

above sea level in metres

- more than 5000m
- 2000 – 5000m
- 1000 – 2000m
- 500 – 1000m
- 200 – 500m
- less than 200 metres
- land below sea level

▲ highest peaks with heights in metres

Scale

One centimetre on the map represents 45 kilometres on the ground.

0   45   90   135km

The Tour de France is a cycle race of about 3600km through France and neighbouring countries. It lasts three weeks.

There has been a church on the rocky island of Mont Saint Michel for more than a thousand years.

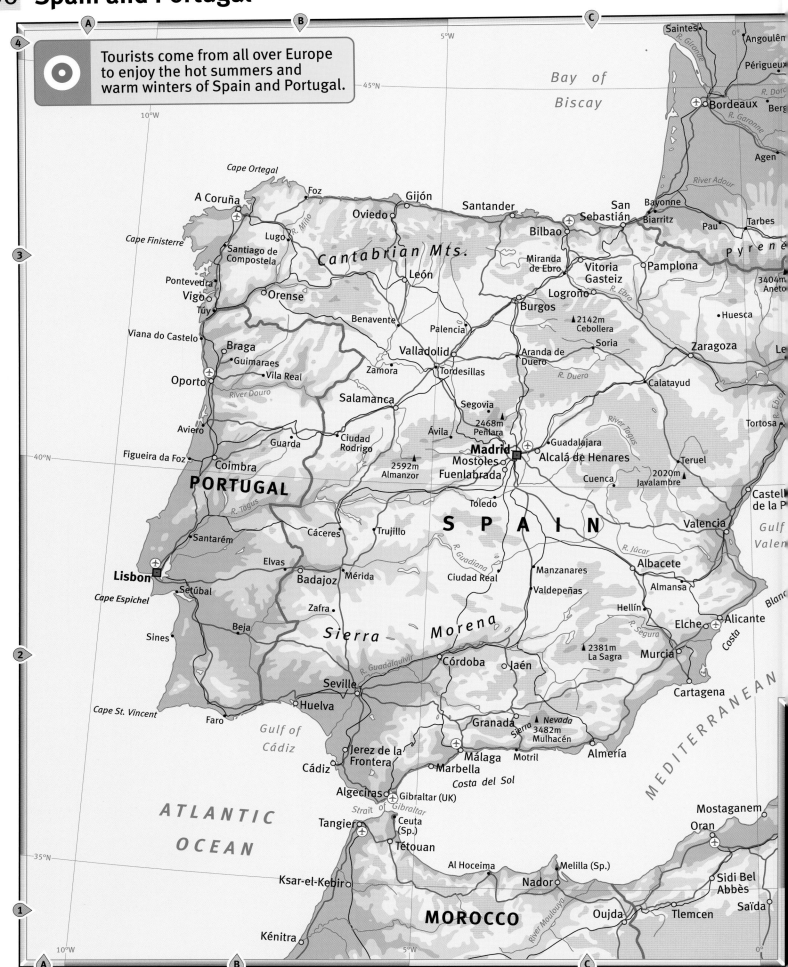

Tourists come from all over Europe to enjoy the hot summers and warm winters of Spain and Portugal.

Bay of Biscay

Cape Ortegal

A Coruña
Foz
Gijón
Santander
San Sebastián
Bayonne
Saintes
Angoulême
Périgueux
Bordeaux
Agen

Cape Finisterre
Lugo
Oviedo
Bilbao
Biarritz
Pau
Tarbes

Santiago de Compostela
Cantabrian Mts.
León
Miranda de Ebro
Vitoria Gasteiz
Pamplona
Pyrenées

Pontevedra
Orense
Benavente
Palencia
Burgos
Logroño
2142m Cebollera
R. Ebro
Huesca
3404m Aneto

Vigo
Túy
Zamora
Valladolid
Tordesillas
Soria
Zaragoza

Viana do Castelo
Braga
Guimaraes
Vila Real
Salamanca
Segovia
Aranda de Duero
R. Duero
Calatayud
Tortosa

Oporto
River Douro
Ávila
2468m Peñlara
2592m Almanzor
Guadalajara
River Tagus

Aviero
Guarda
Ciudad Rodrigo
Madrid
Alcalá de Henares
Teruel

Figueira da Foz
Coimbra
Mostoles
Fuenlabrada
2020m Javalambre

PORTUGAL
R. Tagus
Toledo
Cuenca
Castelló de la P

SPAIN
R. Júcar
Valencia
Gulf of Valen

Santarém
Cáceres
Trujillo
R. Guadiana
Albacete

Lisbon
Elvas
Badajoz
Mérida
Manzanares
Ciudad Real
Valdepeñas
Almansa

Cape Espichel
Setúbal
Zafra
Hellín
R. Segura
Elche
Alicante
Costa Blanc

Sines
Beja
Sierra Morena
2381m La Sagra
Murcia

Córdoba
Jaén
Cartagena

Cape St. Vincent
Faro
R. Guadalquivir
Seville
Granada
Sierra Nevada 3482m Mulhacén
Almería
MEDITERRANEAN

Gulf of Cádiz
Huelva
Jerez de la Frontera
Málaga
Motril
Marbella
Costa del Sol

Cádiz
Algeciras
Gibraltar (UK)
Ceuta (Sp.)

ATLANTIC OCEAN
Tangier
Strait of Gibraltar
Tétouan
Mostaganem
Oran

Ksar-el-Kebir
Al Hoceima
Melilla (Sp.)
Sidi Bel Abbès

MOROCCO
Nador
Oujda
Tlemcen
Saïda

Kénitra
River Moulouya

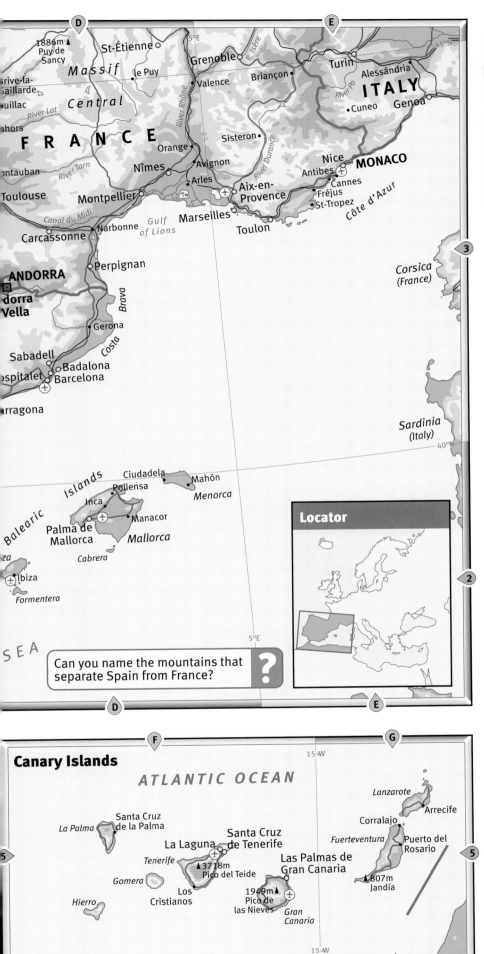

Main map (France, Spain, Italy region)

1886m ▲ Puy de Sancy
St-Étienne
Grenoble
R. Isère
Turin
Alessándria
River Po
Massif
le Puy
Valence
Briançon
ITALY
rive-la-Gaillarde
Central
uillac
ahors
River Lot
Cuneo
Genoa
FRANCE
Sisteron
Orange
Avignon
River Tarn
ntauban
Nîmes
Arles
River Durance
Nice
Antibes
MONACO
Toulouse
Montpellier
Aix-en-Provence
Cannes
Fréjus
St-Tropez
Côte d'Azur
Canal du Midi
Marseilles
Toulon
Narbonne
Gulf of Lions
Carcassonne
5°E
40°N
45°N
Perpignan
ANDORRA
dorra Vella
Corsica (France)
Brava
Gerona
Costa
Sabadell
spitalet
Badalona
Barcelona
rragona
Sardinia (Italy)
40°N
Islands
Ciudadela
Mahón
Pollensa
Inca
Menorca
Balearic
Manacor
Palma de Mallorca
Mallorca
za
Cabrera
Ibiza
Formentera
5°E

SEA

Can you name the mountains that separate Spain from France? **?**

Locator

Flamenco is a style of music and dance from Andalucia in southern Spain.

Windmills south of Toledo. In a famous Spanish story the knight Don Quixote thought that windmills like these were giants.

Chimneys of a block of flats called Casa Mila in Barcelona. The building was designed by Antoni Gaudi.

Canary Islands

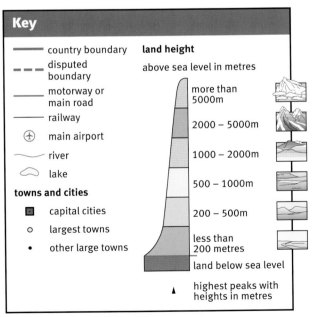

ATLANTIC OCEAN
15°W
Lanzarote
La Palma
Santa Cruz de la Palma
Arrecife
Corralajo
Fuerteventura
Santa Cruz de Tenerife
La Laguna
Puerto del Rosario
Tenerife
▲3718m Pico del Teide
Las Palmas de Gran Canaria
Gomera
Los Cristianos
1949m▲ Pico de las Nieves
807m▲ Jandía
Hierro
Gran Canaria
15°W

Key

——	country boundary
- - -	disputed boundary
——	motorway or main road
——	railway
⊕	main airport
∿	river
⌒	lake

towns and cities

▣	capital cities
○	largest towns
•	other large towns

land height

above sea level in metres

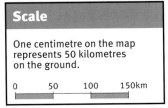

more than 5000m
2000 – 5000m
1000 – 2000m
500 – 1000m
200 – 500m
less than 200 metres
land below sea level

▲ highest peaks with heights in metres

Scale

One centimetre on the map represents 50 kilometres on the ground.

0   50   100   150km

A wide, low plain stretches from the Netherlands through Germany to Poland. To the south lie the high mountains of the Alps.

DENMARK
Esbjerg
Copenhagen
Lund
Malmö
Odense
Fyn
Sjaelland
Bornholm (Denmark)
North Friesian Islands
Flensburg
Kiel
Rügen
Koszalin
Lübeck
Stralsund
Rostock
Szczecin
Schwerin
Gorzów Wielkopols
Friesian Islands
Wilhelmshaven
Emden
Bremerhaven
Hamburg
Den Helder
Leeuwarden
Groningen
R. Elbe
Amsterdam
NETHERLANDS
Leiden
Oldenburg
Bremen
Wittenberge
Brandenburg
Berlin
Hengelo
Osnabrück
Hannover
Potsdam
Zielona Góra
The Hague
Rotterdam
Utrecht
Enschede
Arnhem
Bielefeld
Braunschweig
Magdeburg
R. Weser
Dordrecht
Nijmegen
Münster
GERMANY
Dortmund
Hamm
Paderborn
Harz
Halle
Cottbus
Breda
Tilburg
Duisburg
Oostende
Dunkerque
Bruges
Antwerp
Eindhoven
Essen
Wuppertal
Krefeld
Düsseldorf
Kassel
Leipzig
Riesa
Dresden
Görlitz
Sudet
Legn
Gent
Cologne
Siegen
Erfurt
Gera
Chemnitz
Brussels
Maastricht
Aachen
Bonn
BELGIUM
Lille
Lens
Liège
R. Rhine
Koblenz
Wiesbaden
Frankfurt-am-Main
Fulda
Hof
Cheb
Walbr
Valenciennes
Charleroi
Namur
Ardennes
R. Meuse
Bayreuth
Prague
Hrade Králo
St-Quentin
Amiens
LUXEMBOURG
R. Mosel
Mainz
Würzburg
CZECH REPUBLIC
Charleville-Mézières
Luxembourg
Thionville
Mannheim
R. Main
Nuremberg
Regensburg
Plzen
Kolín
Laon
Reims
Verdun
Metz
Saarbrücken
Heidelberg
Ansbach
Ceské Budějovice
Tábor
Br
R. Oise
R. Marne
Châlons-sur-Marne
Nancy
Heilbronn
Karlsruhe
Stuttgart
Ingolstadt
R. Vltava
Paris
St-Dizier
Strasbourg
Offenburg
River Danube
FRANCE
Fontainebleau
Troyes
Chaumont
R. Rhine
Freiburg
Ulm
Augsburg
Munich
Linz
Vienna
River Seine
Vosges
Tuttlingen
Wels
Auxerre
R. Moselle
Mulhouse
Lake Constance
Memmingen
Salzburg
Wiener Neustadt
Dijon
Belfort
Basel
Winterthur
St. Gallen
Innsbruck
AUSTRIA
Leoben
River Saône
Nevers
Besançon
Zürich
R. Inn
R. Mur
Graz
Beaune
Luzern
Bern
Vaduz
LIECHTENSTEIN
Brenner Pass
Gross Glockner 3798m
R. Drava
Klagenfurt
Mâcon
Jura
Lausanne
SWITZERLAND
Chur
Villach
Villeurbanne
River Allier
Montreux
Jungfrau 4158m
R. Rhône
A L P S
St. Moritz
Bolzano
Dolomites
Maribor
Roanne
Lake Geneva
Geneva
Annecy
Bernina Pass
Kranj
Lyons
Matterhorn 4477m
Lake Maggiore
Trento
Udine
Ljubljana
Clermont-Ferrand
St-Étienne
Chambéry
Mont Blanc 4807m
Aosta
Lake Como
Lake Garda
SLOVENIA
Zag
le Puy
R. Isère
Grenoble
Como
Bérgamo
Vicenza
Treviso
Trieste
Rijeka
Massif Central
Valence
Briançon
Novara
Brescia
Verona
Padua
Venice
Karlovac
River Rhône
Turin
ITALY
Senj
Orange
Piacenza
Cremona
Parma
Módena
Ferrara
River Po
R. Po
Alessándria
Genoa
Reggio nell' 'Emilia
Bologna

D 20°E E 25°E F

BALTIC SEA

LITHUANIA

River Neman

Sovetsk Kaunas Vilnius
Kaliningrad • Marijampole
KALININGRAD
(RUSSIA)

Gdynia
Gdansk Elblag Hrodna Lida
Tczew • Elk
Olsztyn River Neman Baranavichy
3
Bydgoszcz BELARUS
Torun
Wloclawek Bialystok
znan Plock River Pripyat'
Warsaw Brest
P O L A N D Luków
Kalisz Lodz Kovel'
Radom Lublin
Piotrków Luts'k
Trybunalski
Wroclaw Kielce
Czestochowa
R.Oder River Vistula 50°N
Bytom Rzeszow L'viv
Gliwice Sosnowiec Przemysl
Katowice Kraków UKRAINE
ts Ostrava Bielsko-Biala Stryy River Dnestr
Olomouc C A R P A T Ivano-Frankivs'k
Zilina Presov H
SLOVAKIA Kosice I
Uzhgorod A
Miskolc N Satu Mare
Bratislava Nyíregyháza S Baia Mare 2
Vác Debrecen
Györ Budapest R. Tisza
Székesfehérvár Cegléd Oradea
Kecskemét Cluj-Napoca Târgu Mures
Lake Turda
Balaton H U N G A R Y
Szeged Arad
Pécs Subotica Timisoara
River Drava
CROATIA Osijek Novi Sad
Slavonski Vrsac
nja Luka Brod R. Danube 45°N
BOSNIA- R. Sava Belgrade
ERZEGOVINA

55°N

Can you name some countries that share the Alps? **?**

Locator

Key

——	country boundary	
– – –	disputed boundary	
——	motorway or main road	
——	railway	
⊕	main airport	
～	river	
⌒	lake	

towns and cities

◼ capital cities
○ largest towns
• other large towns

land height
above sea level in metres

more than 5000m	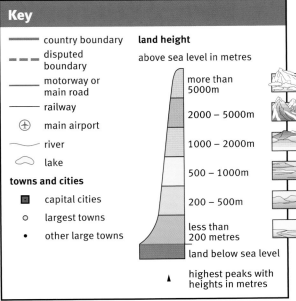
2000 – 5000m	
1000 – 2000m	
500 – 1000m	
200 – 500m	
less than 200 metres	

land below sea level

▲ highest peaks with heights in metres

Scale

One centimetre on the map represents 50 kilometres on the ground.

0   50   100   150km

Beach chairs on the Frisian Islands. They are all turned to face away from the wind.

This clock in Prague is 600 years old. As well as telling the time it also shows the position of the sun, moon and stars.

Neuschwanstein Castle in Germany has given many artists and film makers ideas about how castles should be shown in fairytales.

© Oxford University Press

SWITZERLAND
Jura
Lausanne
Montreux
Jungfrau
4158m
Chur
A L P S
Brenner
Pass
3798m
Gross Glockner
AUSTRIA
Graz
Székesfehérvár
River Mur
Lake
Balaton
HUNGARY
Geneva
Annecy
Lake
Geneva
R. Rhône
St. Moritz
Bernina
Pass
Bolzano
Dolomites
Klagenfurt
Villach
R. Drava
Maribor
Varazdin
Pécs
4807m
Mont Blanc
4477m
Matterhorn
Lake
Maggiore
Lake
Como
Trento
Kranj
Ljubljana
SLOVENIA
Zagreb
CROATIA
Osijek
Slavonski
Brod
FRANCE
Aosta
Novara
Como
Monza
Bérgamo
Brescia
Lake
Garda
Vicenza
Verona
Treviso
Padua
Udine
Trieste
Rijeka
Karlovac
Briançon
Turin
Milan
R. Po
Alessándria
Piacenza
Cremona
Parma
Ferrara
R. Po
Venice
Senj
Banja Luka
Doboj
Tuzl
3841m
Mt. Viso
Cuneo
Reggio nell'
Emilia
Módena
Bologna
Ravenna
ADRIATIC
Zadar
BOSNIA-HERZEGOVINA
Zenica
Genoa
A P P E N N I N E S
Forlí
Rimini
Sarajev
Nice
Antibes
MONACO
La Spézia
Prato
Florence
SAN
MARINO
Ancona
SEA
Split
Mostar
Cannes
Fréjus
St-Tropez
Côte d'Azur
LIGURIAN
SEA
Pisa
R. Arno
Livorno
Arezzo
Siena
Lake Trasimeno
Perugia
Assisi
ITALY
Terni
R. Tiber
Dinaric Alps
MONTENE
Podgori
Cape Corse
Elba
Lake
Bolsena
Viterbo
L'Aquila
2487m
Mt. Velino
Pescara
Termoli
Dubrovnik
Monte Cinto
2710m
Bastia
Ponte Leccia
Civitavecchia
Rome
Tivoli
Foggia
Bari
Monopoli
Corsica
(France)
Ajaccio
Latina
Cassino
Vesuvius
1277m
R. Ofanto
Bríndisi
Lecce
Bonifacio
Naples
Salerno
Potenza
Táranto
Sassari
Olbia
TYRRHENIAN
Capri
Mt. Pollino
2248m
Gulf of
Táranto
Gallipoli
Otrant
Sardinia
(Italy)
Nuoro
SEA
40°N
Cape Santa
Maria of Leuca
Oristano
R. Tirso
Iglesias
Cágliari
Cape Carbonara
Cosenza
Catanzaro
MEDITERRANEAN
Lipari
Islands
Messina
Reggio di Calabria
IONIAN SEA
Cape Spartivento
Trápani
Palermo
Marsala
Nebrodi Mts.
3323m
Mt. Etna
Sicily
Catania
Agrigento
Caltanissetta
SEA
Siracusa
Cape Passero
Cape Bon
Pantelleria
(Italy)

Locator

Tunis

Can you name the sea that
separates Italy from Croatia?
?

Valletta
MALTA

Italy is shaped like a boot. It looks as though it is kicking Sicily.

D
E
3

Oradea
Kecskemét
Szeged
Arad
Subotica
Timisoara
Deva
Sebes
Sibiu
Brasov
Novi Sad
ROMANIA
Buzau
Vrsac
Ramnica Valcea
Ploiesti
45°N
Belgrade
Pitesti
Drobeta-Turnu-Severin
Bucharest
Craiova
Kragujevac
Caracal
SERBIA
Ruse
River Danube
Pleven
Nis
Balkan Mountains
BULGARIA
Sliven
Pristina
Sofia
Stara Zagora
KOSOVO
Plovdiv
Kumanovo
Rhodope Mountains
Edirne
Skopje
FYRO MACEDONIA
Prilep
Sérres
Xánthi
Thásos
Gelibolu
Tiranë
Bitola
Canakkale
Édessa
40°N
ALBANIA
Kozáni
Thessaloníki
Límnos
Mt. Olympus 2917m
Pindus Mountains
Lésvos
AEGEAN SEA
Ioánnina
Lárisa
Vólos
Chíos
GREECE
Euboea
Lamía
Parnassós 2457m
1
Patras
Kefalloniá
Kórinthos
Piraeus
Athens
Ándros
Peloponnese
Pyrgos
Trípoli
Cyclades
Náxos
Kalamáta
Kythira
Crete
Iráklion
Chaniá
20°E
25°E
30°E

Mount Etna in Sicily is one of the most active volcanoes in the world.

Venice is a city built on islands and joined by waterways.

Key

——	country boundary
- - -	disputed boundary
——	motorway or main road
—	railway
⊕	main airport
~	river
◠	lake

towns and cities

■	capital cities
○	largest towns
•	other large towns

land height

above sea level in metres

- more than 5000m
- 2000 – 5000m
- 1000 – 2000m
- 500 – 1000m
- 200 – 500m
- less than 200 metres
- land below sea level

▲ highest peaks with heights in metres

Scale

One centimetre on the map represents 50 kilometres on the ground.

0   50   100   150km

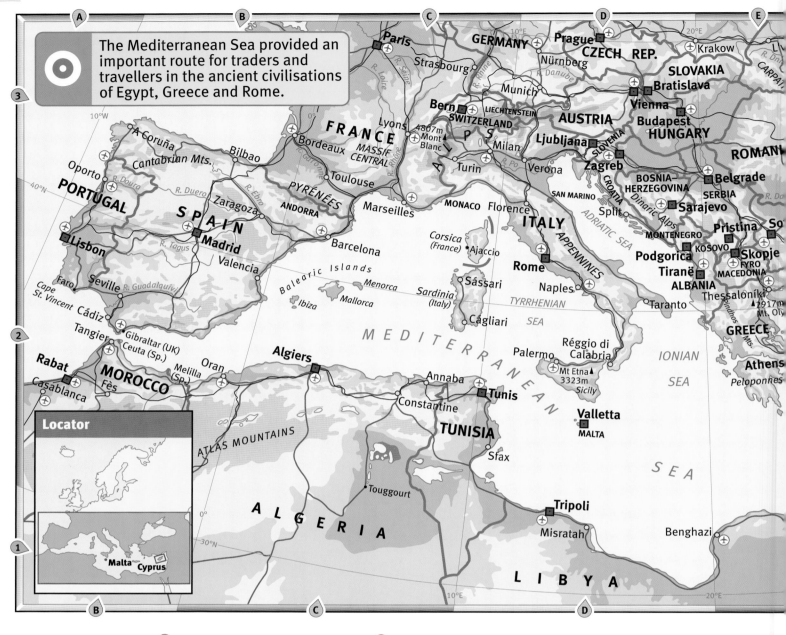

The Mediterranean Sea provided an important route for traders and travellers in the ancient civilisations of Egypt, Greece and Rome.

Locator

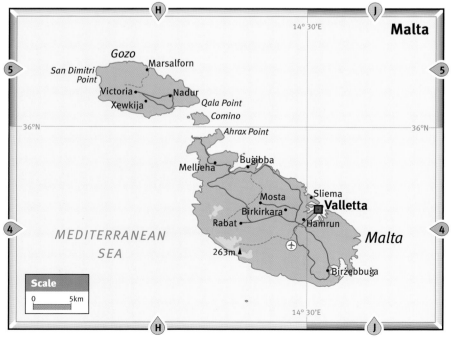

Malta

Gozo

San Dimitri Point
Marsalforn
Victoria
Nadur
Xewkija
Qala Point
Comino
Ahrax Point

Mellieħa
Buġibba
Mosta
Sliema
Birkirkara
Valletta
Rabat
Ħamrun

MEDITERRANEAN SEA

Malta

263m

Birżebbuġa

Scale
0   5km

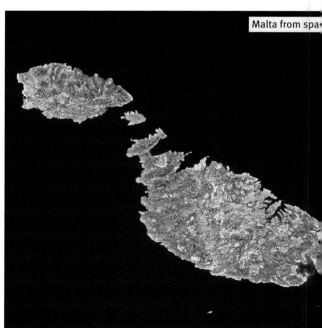

Malta from space

© Oxford University Press
Conical Orthomorphic Projection

Key

——	country boundary
- - -	disputed boundary
——	motorway or main road
——	railway
⊕	main airport
~~	river
⌒	lake

towns and cities

◼	capital cities
○	largest towns
•	other large towns

land height

above sea level in metres

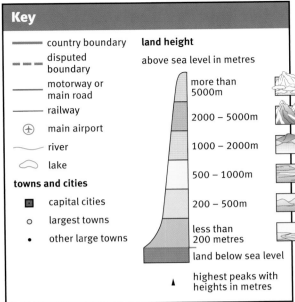

- more than 5000m
- 2000 – 5000m
- 1000 – 2000m
- 500 – 1000m
- 200 – 500m
- less than 200 metres
- land below sea level

▲ highest peaks with heights in metres

Scale

One centimetre on the map represents 150 kilometres on the ground.

0   150   300   450km

Can you name three of the Balearic Islands? ❓

The Amalfi coast south of Naples has rocky cliffs and tiny bays.

Cyprus

MEDITERRANEAN SEA

Cape Andreas
Risokarpaso
Cape Kormakiti
Kyrenia
Cape Arnaoutis
Morphou
Lefkoniko
Polis
Nicosia ◼ ⊕
Famagusta
Mt. Olympus ▲ 1951m
Larnaca
Troodos Mountains
Cape Greco
Paphos
Limassol
Cape Gata

Scale

0   25km

Alexandria is Egypt's largest sea port. Can you find it on the map?

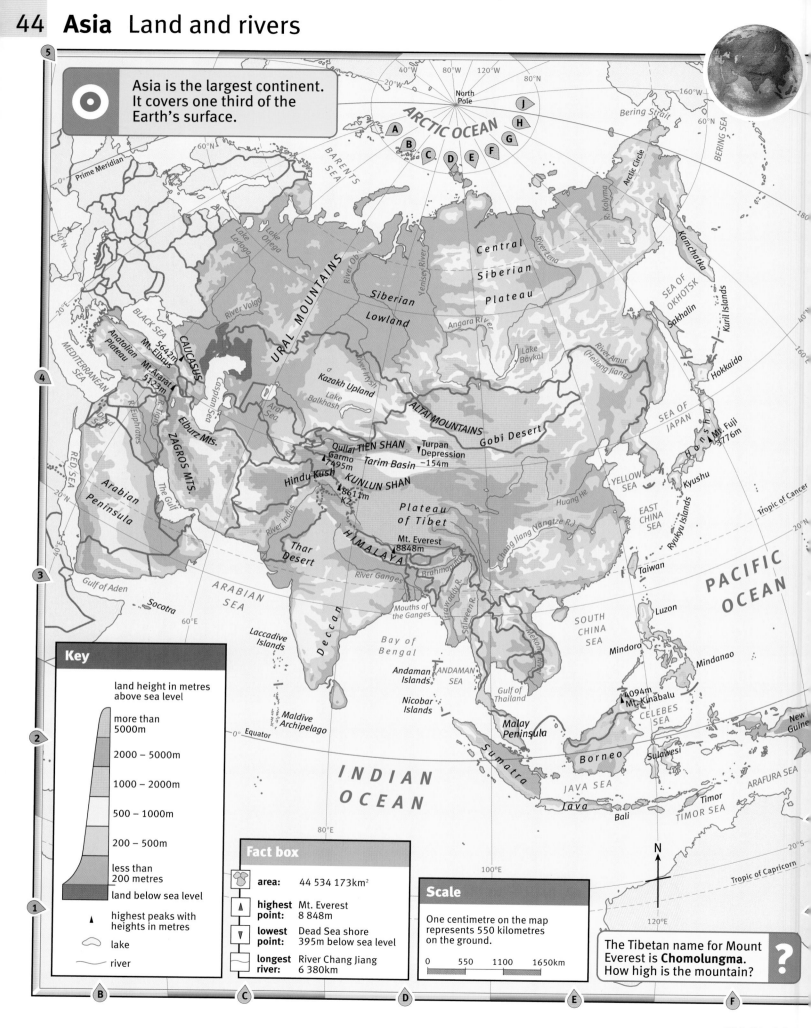

Asia is the largest continent. It covers one third of the Earth's surface.

Key

land height in metres above sea level

more than 5000m

2000 – 5000m

1000 – 2000m

500 – 1000m

200 – 500m

less than 200 metres

land below sea level

▲ highest peaks with heights in metres

lake

river

Fact box

	area:	44 534 173km²
▲	**highest point**	Mt. Everest 8 848m
▼	**lowest point:**	Dead Sea shore 395m below sea level
	longest river:	River Chang Jiang 6 380km

Scale

One centimetre on the map represents 550 kilometres on the ground.

0   550   1100   1650km

The Tibetan name for Mount Everest is **Chomolungma**. How high is the mountain?

?

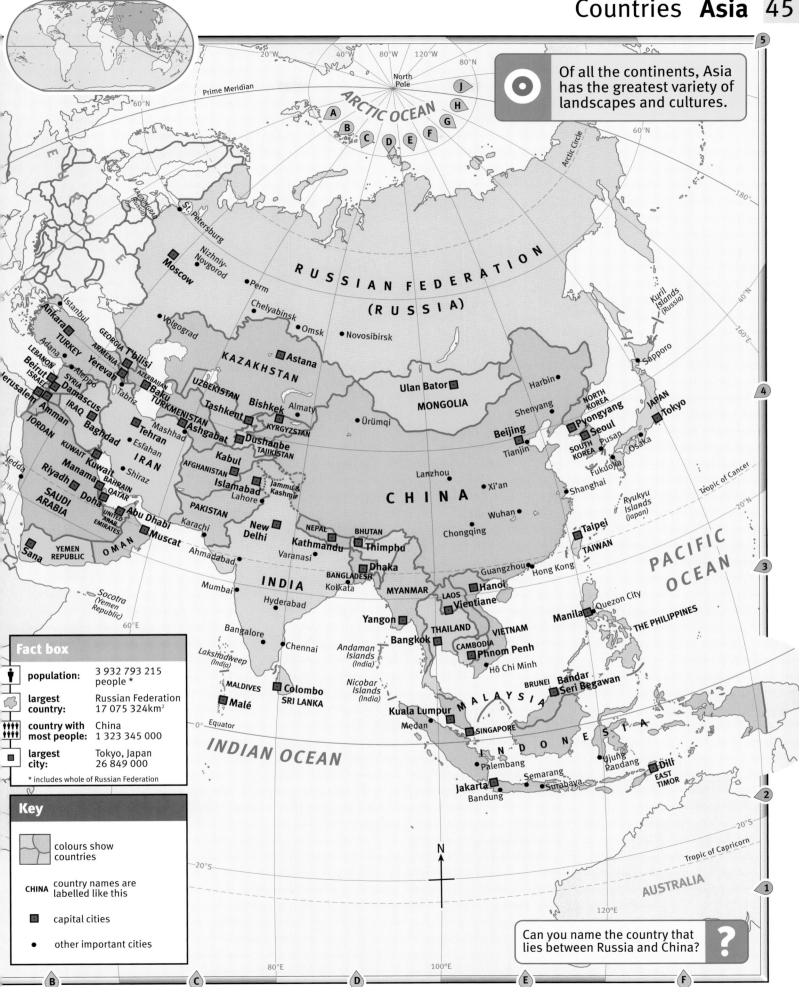

5 | **4** | **3** | **2** | **1**

Of all the continents, Asia has the greatest variety of landscapes and cultures.

North Pole

ARCTIC OCEAN

Prime Meridian
60°N

A
B
C
D
E
F
G
H
J

Arctic Circle
60°N
180°
40°N
160°E

KALININGRAD (Russia)
St. Petersburg

Moscow
Nizhniy-Novgorod
Perm

R U S S I A N   F E D E R A T I O N

(R U S S I A)

Chelyabinsk
Volgograd
Omsk
Novosibirsk

Kuril Islands (Russia)

Istanbul
Ankara
TURKEY
GEORGIA
ARMENIA
T'bilisi
AZERBAIJAN
Yerevan
Baku
TURKMENISTAN
Adana
Aleppo
LEBANON
SYRIA
Beirut
Damascus
ISRAEL
IRAQ
Jerusalem
Amman
Baghdad
JORDAN
Tehran
Mashhad
Esfahan
IRAN
Shiraz
KUWAIT
Kuwait
Manama
BAHRAIN
Riyadh
Doha
QATAR
SAUDI ARABIA
UNITED ARAB EMIRATES
Abu Dhabi
Muscat
OMAN
Jedda
Sana
YEMEN REPUBLIC

KAZAKHSTAN
Astana

UZBEKISTAN
Tashkent
Bishkek
Almaty
KYRGYZSTAN
Ashgabat
Dushanbe
TAJIKISTAN
Kabul
AFGHANISTAN
Tabriz
Islamabad
Lahore
Jammu & Kashmir
PAKISTAN
Karachi
New Delhi

Ürümqi

Ulan Bator
MONGOLIA

Harbin
Shenyang

NORTH KOREA
Pyongyang
Seoul
SOUTH KOREA
Pusan
Beijing
Tianjin

Sapporo
JAPAN
Tokyo
Fukuoka
Osaka

Lanzhou
Xi'an
C H I N A
Wuhan
Chongqing
Shanghai

Ryukyu Islands (Japan)

Tropic of Cancer
20°N

NEPAL
Kathmandu
BHUTAN
Thimphu
Ahmadabad
Varanasi
Dhaka
BANGLADESH
Kolkata
Mumbai
I N D I A
Hyderabad
MYANMAR

Guangzhou
Hong Kong

Taipei
TAIWAN

PACIFIC OCEAN

Hanoi
LAOS
Vientiane
VIETNAM

Socotra (Yemen Republic)
60°E

Bangalore
Chennai
Lakshadweep (India)

Yangon
THAILAND
Bangkok
CAMBODIA
Phnom Penh
Hô Chi Minh

Manila
Quezon City
THE PHILIPPINES

Andaman Islands (India)

MALDIVES
Malé
Colombo
SRI LANKA

Nicobar Islands (India)

BRUNEI
Bandar Seri Begawan

Kuala Lumpur
Medan
SINGAPORE
M A L A Y S I A

I N D O N E S I A

Ujung Pandang
Dili
EAST TIMOR

0° Equator

INDIAN OCEAN

Palembang
Semarang
Jakarta
Bandung
Surabaya

20°S

20°S

N

Tropic of Capricorn

AUSTRALIA

120°E

Fact box

🧍	population:	3 932 793 215 people *
🗺	largest country:	Russian Federation 17 075 324km²
👥	country with most people:	China 1 323 345 000
⬛	largest city:	Tokyo, Japan 26 849 000

* includes whole of Russian Federation

Key

colours show countries

CHINA country names are labelled like this

⬛ capital cities

• other important cities

Can you name the country that lies between Russia and China? **?**

B | **C** | **D** | **E** | **F**

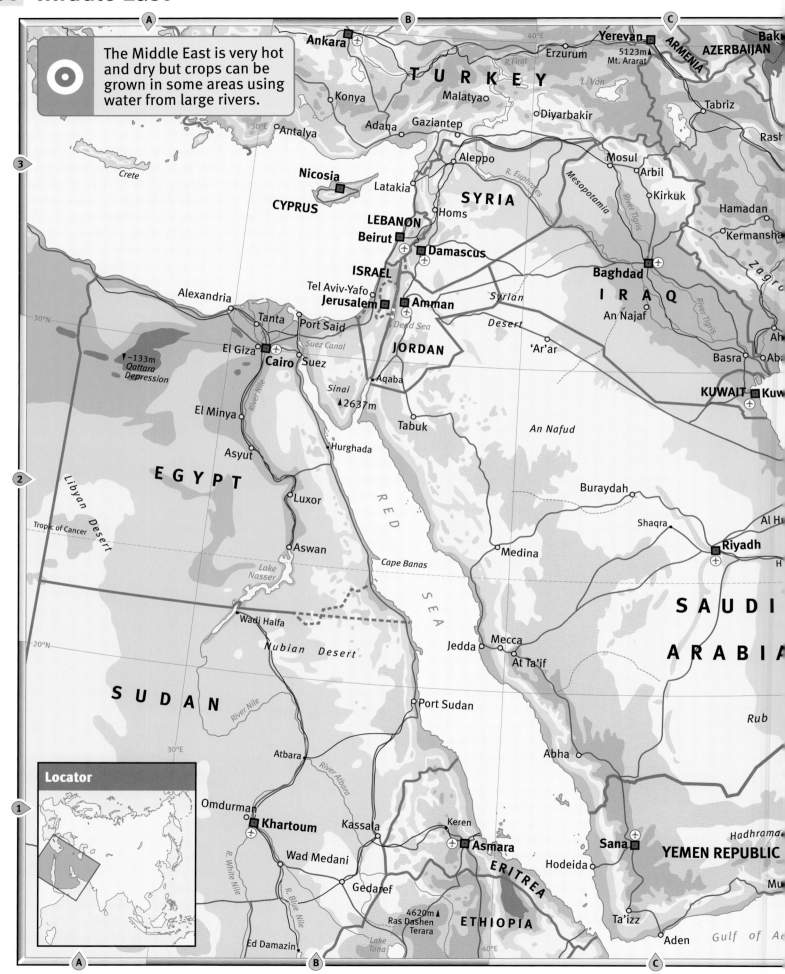

The Middle East is very hot and dry but crops can be grown in some areas using water from large rivers.

TURKEY

Ankara

Konya

Antalya

Adana

Gaziantep

Erzurum

Malatyao

Diyarbakir

Yerevan 5123m Mt. Ararat

ARMENIA **AZERBAIJAN** Bak

L. Van

Tabriz

Rash

Crete

Nicosia

CYPRUS

Latakia

Aleppo

R. Euphrates

Mosul

Arbil

Kirkuk

Mesopotamia

River Tigris

Hamadan

Kermansha

SYRIA

Homs

LEBANON

Beirut

Damascus

ISRAEL

Tel Aviv-Yafo

Jerusalem

Amman

Dead Sea

Syrlan

Desert

Baghdad

I R A Q

An Najaf

Za

River Tigris

Ah

Basra

Aba

Alexandria

Tanta

Port Said

El Giza

Cairo Suez

Suez Canal

30°N

−133m Qattara Depression

JORDAN

Aqaba

'Ar'ar

KUWAIT Kuw

Sinai ▲2637m

Tabuk

An Nafud

E G Y P T

El Minya

Asyut

Libyan Desert

Tropic of Cancer

Luxor

Aswan

Lake Nasser

R
E
D

S
E
A

Hurghada

Cape Banas

Medina

Buraydah

Shaqra

Al Hi

Riyadh

H

S A U D I

A R A B I A

Rub

Wadi Halfa

Nubian Desert

Jedda

Mecca

At Ta'if

Abha

20°N

S U D A N

River Nile

Port Sudan

30°E

Atbara

River Atbara

Omdurman

Khartoum

Kassala

Keren

Asmara

Sana

YEMEN REPUBLIC

Hadhrama

Mu

R. White Nile

Wad Medani

R. Blue Nile

Gedaref

4620m ▲
Ras Dashen Terara

ETHIOPIA

Lake Tana

ERITREA

Hodeida

Ta'izz

Aden

Gulf of A

40°E

Ed Damazin

Locator

© Oxford University Pres
Conical Orthomorphic Projectio

TURKMENISTAN

Krasnovodsk

Chardzhev

Ashgabat

Caspian Sea

R. Hari Rud

Mashhad

Sabzevar

Mountains

▲Damavand 5671m

Tehran

Herat

Qom

Dasht-e-Kavir

AFGHANISTAN

IRAN

Birjand

Farah

Isfahan

Yazd

Dasht - e Lut

River Helmand

Mountains

Kerman

30°N

Chagai Hills

Shiraz

Zahedan

Bushehr

Khash

Baluchistan

Gulf

Bandar-e 'Abbas

R. Kech

Dammam

Makran

BAHRAIN

OMAN

Manama

QATAR

Chah Bahar

Doha

Dubai

Gulf of Oman

Abu Dhabi

Tropic of Cancer

UNITED ARAB EMIRATES

Muscat

▲3018m Mt. Akhdar

Sur

ARABIAN SEA

O M A N

20°N

Masirah

Cape Madrakah

• Kuria Muria Is.

Salalah

60°E

Cape Fartak

Al Masilah

A R A B I A N SEA

Socotra (Yemen Republic)

Can you name the land that lies between the rivers Tigris and Euphrates? ?

Key

——	country boundary
- - -	disputed boundary
——	motorway or main road
——	railway
⊕	main airport
⌇	river
◠	lake

towns and cities

▣	capital cities
○	largest towns
•	other large towns

land height

above sea level in metres

more than 5000m

2000 – 5000m

1000 – 2000m

500 – 1000m

200 – 500m

less than 200 metres

land below sea level

▲ highest peaks with heights in metres

Scale

One centimetre on the map represents 120 kilometres on the ground.

0   120   240   360km

Each year, thousands of Muslims join in a pilgrimage to Mecca.

Nakhal Fort in Oman is one of the best castles in the world.

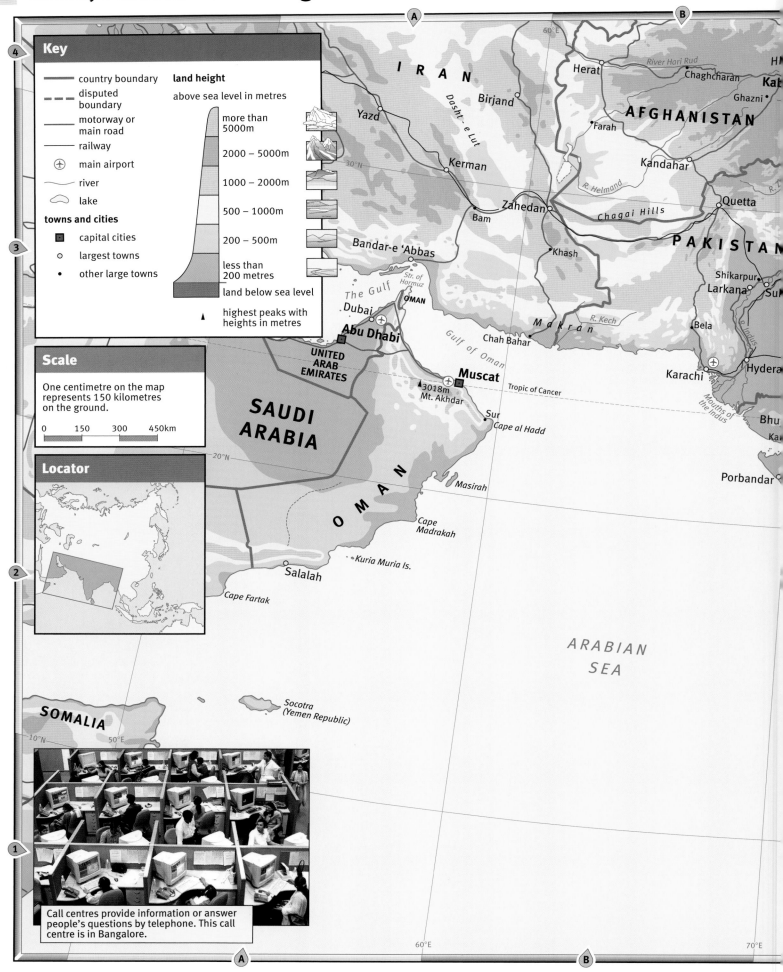

Key

———	country boundary
- - -	disputed boundary
———	motorway or main road
———	railway
⊕	main airport
～～	river
～～	lake

towns and cities

▣	capital cities
○	largest towns
•	other large towns

land height

above sea level in metres

more than 5000m

2000 – 5000m

1000 – 2000m

500 – 1000m

200 – 500m

less than 200 metres

land below sea level

▲ highest peaks with heights in metres

Scale

One centimetre on the map represents 150 kilometres on the ground.

0   150   300   450km

Locator

IRAN

AFGHANISTAN

Herat
Chaghcharan
Kab
Ghazni

River Hari Rud

Birjand

Yazd

Dasht-e Lut

Kandahar

Farah

R. Helmand

Kerman

Bam

Zahedan

Chagai Hills

Quetta

Khash

PAKISTAN

Bandar-e 'Abbas

Shikarpur
Larkana
Su

Str. of Hormuz

The Gulf

Makran

R. Kech

Bela

OMAN

Dubai

R. Indus

Abu Dhabi

Gulf of Oman

Chah Bahar

UNITED ARAB EMIRATES

Karachi

Hydera

Muscat

SAUDI ARABIA

▲ 3018m
Mt. Akhdar

Tropic of Cancer

Mouths of the Indus

Sur
Cape al Hadd

Bhu

Porbandar

Ka

Masirah

OMAN

Cape Madrakah

• Kuria Muria Is.

ARABIAN SEA

Salalah

Cape Fartak

SOMALIA

Socotra
(Yemen Republic)

10°N
50°E

60°E

70°E

20°N

30°N

60°E

Call centres provide information or answer people's questions by telephone. This call centre is in Bangalore.

India is an important centre of the computer software industry. Several million people work at making computer programs.

Mumbai is sometimes called **Bollywood**. Can you find out what are made there?

C H I N A

I N D I A

BANGLADESH

MYANMAR (BURMA)

SRI LANKA

BHUTAN

NEPAL

JAMMU AND KASHMIR

HIMALAYA

WESTERN GHATS

EASTERN GHATS

Deccan

Thar Desert

PAMIRS
TAJIKISTAN

INDIAN OCEAN

Bay of Bengal

ANDAMAN SEA

Andaman Islands

Laccadive Islands

Mouths of the Ganges

Mouths of the Irrawaddy

Gulf of Khambhat

Arakan Yoma

Tropic of Cancer

Khorog
7690m
Gilgit
K2 (Qogir Feng, Godwin Austen) 8611m
Islamabad
Rawalpindi
Srinagar
Leh
Jammu
Gujranwala
Lahore
Amritsar
Faisalabad
Chandigarh
Ludhiana
Multan
Ghazi Khan
Bahawalpur
Bikaner
New Delhi
Delhi
Meerut
Dehra Dun
Rutog
Bareilly
Jaipur
Agra
Lucknow
Gorakhpur
Annapurna 8091m
Kathmandu
Mount Everest 8848m
Lhaze
Lhasa
Nyingchi
Thimphu
Dibrugarh
Darjiling
Guwahati
Nagaon
Shillong
Imphal
Jodhpur
Kota
Gwalior
Kanpur
Jhansi
Allahabad
Varanasi
Patna
Muzaffarpur
Bhagalpur
Dhaka
Murwara
Dhanbad
Asanol
Ahmadabad
Bhopal
Indore
Jamshedpur
Kolkata
Khulna
Chittagong
Monywa
Mandalay
Vadodara
Bharuch
Jabalpur
Bilaspur
Kharagpur
Surat
Burhanpur
Raipur
Sambalpur
Nashik
Dhule
Amravati
Cuttack
Sittwe
Aurangabad
Nagpur
Chandrapur
Brahmapur
Sandoway
Pye
Pune
Nizamabad
Yangon
Bassein
Solapur
Hyderabad
Vishakhapatnam
Kolhapur
Bijapur
Raichur
Rajahmundry
Belgaum
Vijayawada
Bellary
Nellore
Mangalore
Bangalore
Vellore
Chennai
Mysore
Pondicherry
Calicut
Salem
Coimbatore
Tiruchchirappalli
Cochin
Madurai
Quilon
Trivandrum
Nagercoil
Jaffna
Trincomalee
Batticaloa
Puttalam
Colombo
Kandy
Badulla
Galle
Port Blair

Rivers: R. Indus, R. Jhelum, River Sutlej, Chenab, R. Yamuna, River Ganges, R. Banas, R. Chambal, R. Son, R. Gandak, R. Gomti, R. Narmada, R. Tapi, Gandhi Sagar, Hirakud Reservoir, R. Mahanadi, R. Godavari, R. Indravati, R. Bhima, R. Krishna, R. Pennet, Brahmaputra R, River Chindwin, Irrawaddy R, Arakan Yoma, Yarlung Zangbo (Tsangpo R.), Lancang Jiang (Mekong R.), Nu Jiang (Salween R.)

80°E 90°E 30°N 20°N 10°N

© Oxford University Press

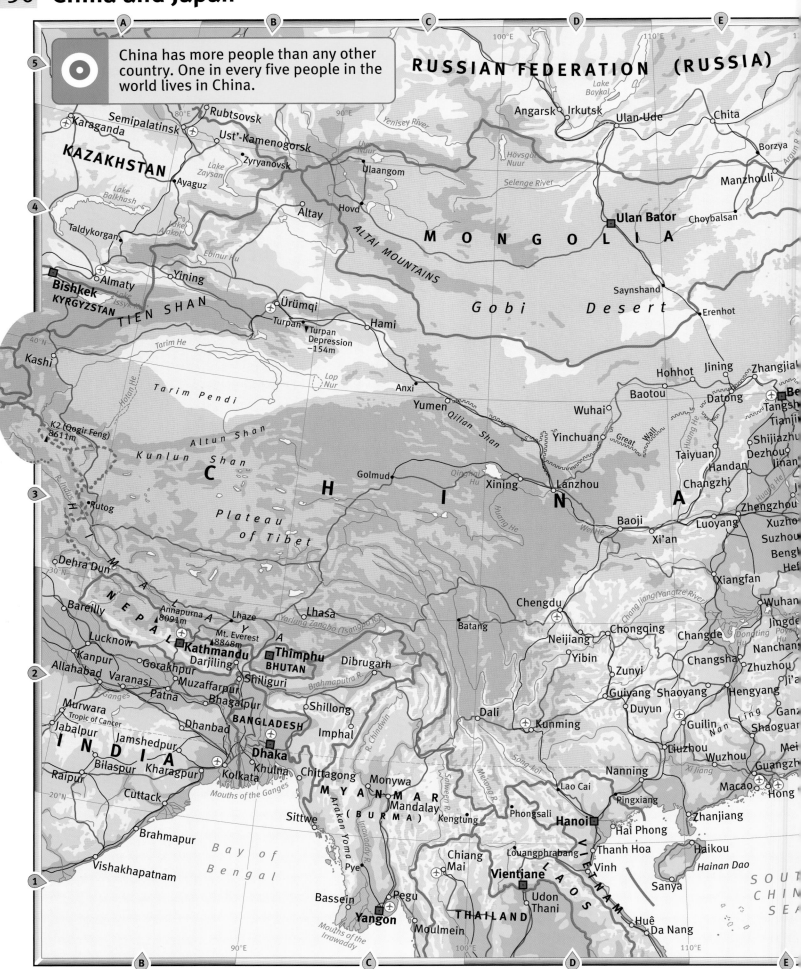

China has more people than any other country. One in every five people in the world lives in China.

RUSSIAN FEDERATION (RUSSIA)

Lake Baykal

Angarsk Irkutsk Ulan-Ude Chita Borzya

Karaganda Semipalatinsk Rubtsovsk Manzhouli

KAZAKHSTAN Ust'-Kamenogorsk

Zyryanovsk Hövsgöl Nuur Uv Nuur

Ayaguz Ulaangom

Lake Zaysan Altay Hovd Choybalsan

Lake Balkhash M O N G O L I A Ulan Bator

Taldykorgan Lake Alakol' Selenge River

Bishkek Almaty Yining Saynshand

KYRGYZSTAN Gobi Desert

TIEN SHAN Ürümqi Erenhot

Kashi Turpan Hami

Turpan Depression −154m

Tarim He Hohhot Jining Zhangjia

Tarim Pendi Lop Nur Anxi Baotou Datong Be

Hotan He Yumen Qilian Shan Wuhai Tangsh

K2 (Qogir Feng) 8611m Golmud Yinchuan Great Wall Taiyuan

Kunlun Shan Qinghai Hu Xining Lanzhou Handan Jinan

Rutog Altun Shan C H I N A Changzhi Dezhou

Plateau of Tibet Huang He Baoji Zhengzhou

R. Indus Baoji Xi'an Luoyang Xuzho

Dehra Dun Wen He Suzho

Bareilly Lhaze Lhasa Xiangfan Beng

Annapurna 8091m Chengdu Chang Jiang (Yangtze River) Hef

NEPAL Yarlung Zangbo (Tsangpo R.) Batang Chongqing Changde Wuhan

Lucknow Mt. Everest 8848m Neijiang Dongting Hu Nanchan

Kanpur Kathmandu Thimphu Dibrugarh Yibin Jingde

Gorakhpur BHUTAN Zunyi Changsha Zhuzhou

Allahabad Darjiling Shiliguri Brahmaputra R. Guiyang Shaoyang Hengyang Ji'a

Varanasi Muzaffarpur Duyun

Patna Bhagalpur Shillong Dali Kunming Guilin Shaoguar Ganz

Murwara Dhanbad BANGLADESH Imphal Nan Ling

Jabalpur Tropic of Cancer Liuzhou Wuzhou Mei

Jamshedpur Dhaka R. Chindwin Nanning Macao Guangzh

Bilaspur Kharagpur Khulna Chittagong Monywa Lao Cai Pingxiang Hong

Raipur I N D I A Kolkata Mouths of the Ganges M Y A N M A R Mandalay Phongsali Zhanjiang

Cuttack Sittwe Arakan Yoma (B U R M A) Kengtung Hanoi Hai Phong Haikou

Brahmapur Mekong R. Song-koi Thanh Hoa Hainan Dao

Vishakhapatnam Bay of Bengal Pye Chiang Mai Louangphrabang Vinh Sanya

Bassein Pegu VIENTIANE L A O S Udon Thani Huê SOUT CHIN SEA

Yangon Moulmein THAILAND Da Nang

Mouths of the Irrawaddy Irrawaddy R. V I E T N A M

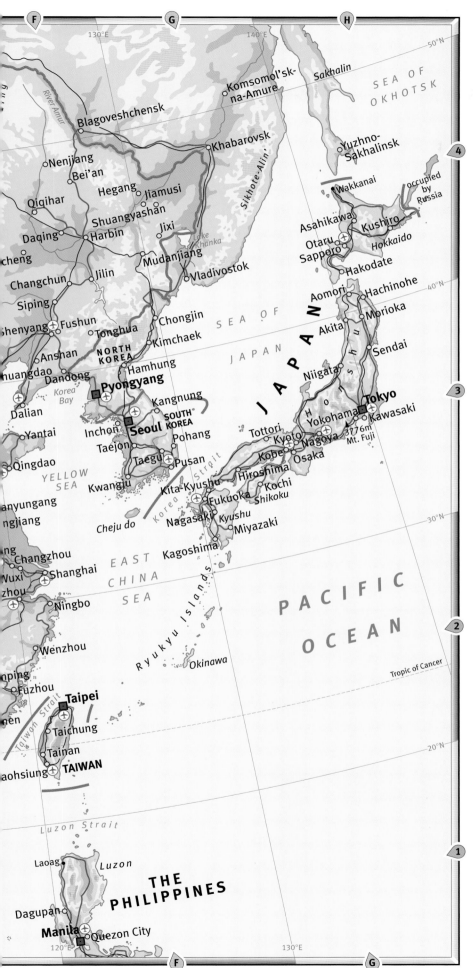

More and more of the things people use are made in Chinese factories.

Key

——	country boundary
– – –	disputed boundary
——	motorway or main road
——	railway
⊕	main airport
～	river
⌒	lake

towns and cities

■	capital cities
○	largest towns
•	other large towns

land height

above sea level in metres

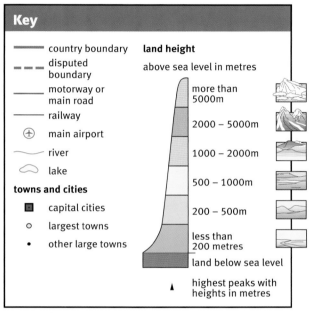

more than 5000m

2000 – 5000m

1000 – 2000m

500 – 1000m

200 – 500m

less than 200 metres

land below sea level

▲ highest peaks with heights in metres

Scale

One centimetre on the map represents 180 kilometres on the ground.

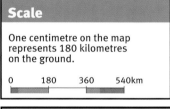

0   180   360   540km

Locator

Japan is a country of islands. Can you name the largest island? **?**

Map labels

River Amur
Blagoveshchensk
Komsomol'sk-na-Amure
Sakhalin
SEA OF OKHOTSK
Nenjiang
Bei'an
Khabarovsk
Hegang
Jiamusi
Qigihar
Shuangyashan
Jixi
Yuzhno-Sakhalinsk
Daqing
Harbin
Lake Khanka
Wakkanai
occupied by Russia
cheng
Changchun
Jilin
Mudanjiang
Asahikawa
Kushiro
Siping
Vladivostok
Otaru
Hokkaido
Sapporo
Shenyang
Fushun
Tonghua
Chongjin
Hakodate
Anshan
Kimchaek
Aomori
Hachinohe
NORTH KOREA
Morioka
huangdao
Dandong
Hamhung
Akita
SEA OF JAPAN
Korea Bay
Pyongyang
Kangnung
Niigata
Sendai
Dalian
Kangnung
SOUTH KOREA
Inchon
Seoul
Tokyo
Yantai
Taejon
Pohang
Yokohama
Kawasaki
Taegu
Tottori
Kyoto
Nagoya
Mt. Fuji 3776m
Qingdao
Pusan
Kobe
Osaka
YELLOW SEA
Kwangju
Hiroshima
Kochi
anyungang
Kita-Kyushu
Shikoku
ngjiang
Fukuoka
Cheju do
Nagasaki
Kyushu
ng
Miyazaki
Changzhou
Kagoshima
EAST CHINA SEA
Wuxi
Shanghai
zhou
Ningbo
Ryukyu Islands
PACIFIC OCEAN
Wenzhou
Okinawa
nping
Fuzhou
Tropic of Cancer
en
Taipei
Taichung
Taiwan Strait
Tainan
TAIWAN
aohsiung
Luzon Strait
Laoag
Luzon
THE PHILIPPINES
Dagupan
Manila
Quezon City

F G H
130°E 140°E 50°N
40°N
30°N
20°N
120°E 130°E

JAPAN
Honshu
Sikhote-Alin

South East Asia is made up of many peninsulas and islands.

Key

——	country boundary
– – –	disputed boundary
——	motorway or main road
——	railway
⊕	main airport
〜	river
◠	lake

towns and cities

■	capital cities
○	largest towns
•	other large towns

land height

above sea level in metres

more than 5000m

2000 – 5000m

1000 – 2000m

500 – 1000m

200 – 500m

less than 200 metres

land below sea level

▲ highest peaks with heights in metres

Scale

One centimetre on the map represents 170 kilometres on the ground.

0   170   340   510km

Bali is the most popular tourist destination in Indonesia. Can you find it on the map?

Singapore

Scale

0   8km

Locator

Map labels

Chittagong, Monywa, Mandalay, Sittwe, Kengtung, Kunming, Liuzhou, Nanning, Lao Cai, Phongsali, Pingxiang, Hanoi, Hai Phong, Thanh Hoa, CHINA, MYANMAR (BURMA), Chiang Mai, Louangphrabang, Vinh, Pye, Vientiane, Da Nang, Sanya, Pegu, Yangon, Tak, Udon Thani, Savannakhet, Huê, Basseín, Moulmein, THAILAND, Nakhon Ratchasima, Mae Nam Mun, Pakxé, ANDAMAN SEA, Mergui, Bangkok, Sisophon, Batdâmbâng, Siem Reap, Tônlé Sap, Qui Nhon, Gulf of Thailand, CAMBODIA, Da Lat, Nha Trang, Ko Samui, Phnom Penh, Rach Gia, Cân Tho, Hô Chi Minh, Mouths of the Mekong, Phuket, Nakhon Si Thammarat, Hat Yai, Banda Aceh, Alor Setar, Kota Bharu, George Town, MALAYSIA, Ipoh, Kuala Terengganu, Pematangsiantar, Medan, Kuantan, Natuna Besar, Kuala Lumpur, Sumatra, Nias, Pekanbaru, Johor Bahru, SINGAPORE, Sambas, Kuching, Padang, Lingga Islands, Pontianak, Mentawi Islands, Jambi, Bangka, Barisan Mountains, 3805m Mt. Kerinci, Palembang, Belitung, Karimata Strait, Tanjungkarang-Telukbetung, INDONESIA, BORNEO, Jakarta, Bogor, Cirebon, Semarang, Bandung, Yogyakarta, Surakarta, Java, INDIAN OCEAN, Christmas I. (Austl.)

Mouths of the Irrawaddy, Arakan Yoma, Chindwin, Irrawaddy River, Salween R., Mekong R., Song-koi, Xi Jiang, Strait of Malacca

Singapore inset

MALAYSIA, 104°00'E, R. Johor, Johor Bahru, Pasir Gudang, Woodlands, Straits of Johor, Ubin, Tekong, Changi, Mt. Timah 162m, SINGAPORE, Jurong, Singapore, Katong, Tuas, Jurong, Sentosa, Straits of Singapore

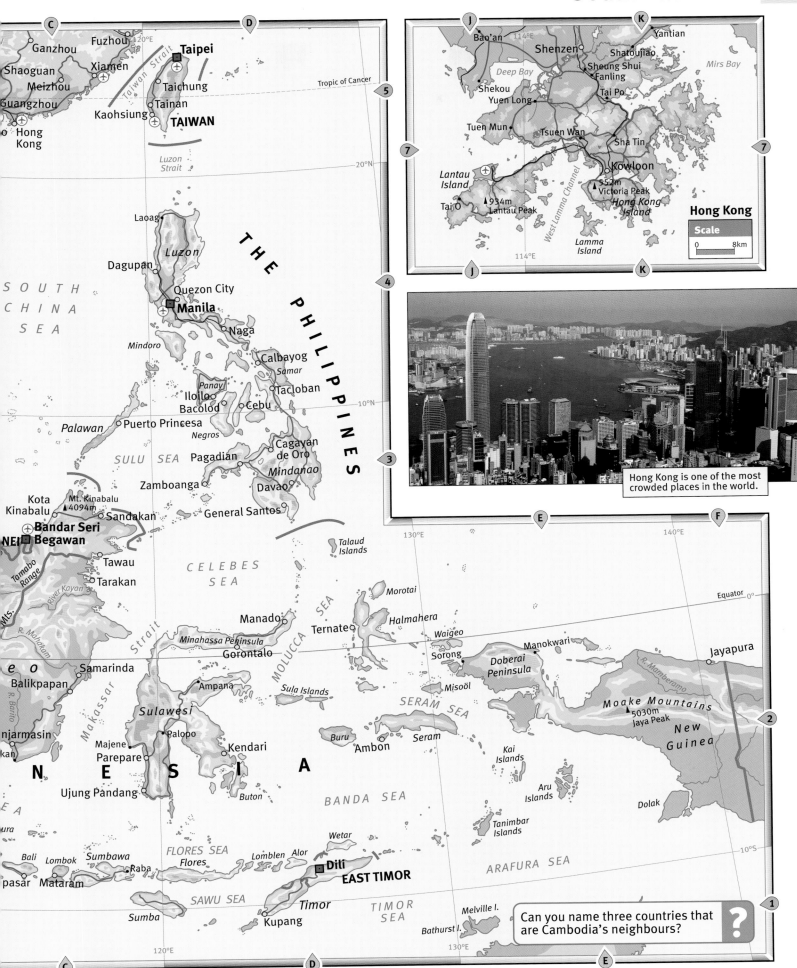

C
Ganzhou
Fuzhou
120°E
Shaoguan
Xiamen
Meizhou
Guangzhou
o Hong
Kong

D
Taipei
Taichung
Tropic of Cancer
5
Tainan
Kaohsiung
TAIWAN

Luzon Strait

20°N

Laoag
Luzon
Dagupan
Quezon City
Manila
Naga
Mindoro
Calbayog
Samar
Panay
Iloilo
Tacloban
Bacolod
Cebu
Palawan
Puerto Princesa
Negros
Cagayan de Oro
SULU SEA
Pagadian
Mindanao
Zamboanga
Davao
Kota Kinabalu
Mt. Kinabalu ▲4094m
General Santos
Sandakan
Bandar Seri
NEI **Begawan**
Tamabo Range
Tawau
Tarakan

SOUTH CHINA SEA

THE PHILIPPINES

10°N

3

Talaud Islands

CELEBES SEA

Morotai

Manado
MOLUCCA SEA
Ternate
Halmahera
Minahassa Peninsula
Gorontalo
Waigeo
Sorong
Manokwari
Doberai Peninsula
Jayapura
Equator 0°
R. Mamberamo
Samarinda
Ampana
Misoöl
SERAM SEA
Balikpapan
R. Barito
Sula Islands
Moake Mountains
▲5030m
Jaya Peak
R. Mahakam
Sulawesi
Palopo
Buru
Seram
New Guinea
2
njarmasin
Ambon
Majene
Kendari
Kai Islands
Parepare
N E S I A
Ujung Pandang
Buton
BANDA SEA
Aru Islands
Dolak
Tanimbar Islands
Makassar Strait

e o
R e o

10°S

Wetar
FLORES SEA
Bali
Lombok
Sumbawa
Lomblen Alor
Raba
Flores
Dili
EAST TIMOR
pasar Mataram
ARAFURA SEA
Sumba
SAWU SEA
Timor
TIMOR SEA
Kupang
Melville I.

1

Borneo
Mts.
R. Kayan

130°E

140°E

E

F

Can you name three countries that are Cambodia's neighbours? **?**

120°E

130°E

C

D

E

Hong Kong map (inset, top right):

J
Bao'an
114°E
Shenzen
Shatoujiao
Yantian
Sheung Shui
Fanling
Mirs Bay
Deep Bay
Tai Po
Shekou
Yuen Long
Tsuen Wan
Tai O
Sha Tin
Kowloon
Tuen Mun
552m
Victoria Peak
Hong Kong Island
Lantau Island
▲934m
Lantau Peak
West Lamma Channel
Lamma Island

K

7

7

Hong Kong

Scale
0   8km

114°E

J

K

Hong Kong is one of the most crowded places in the world.

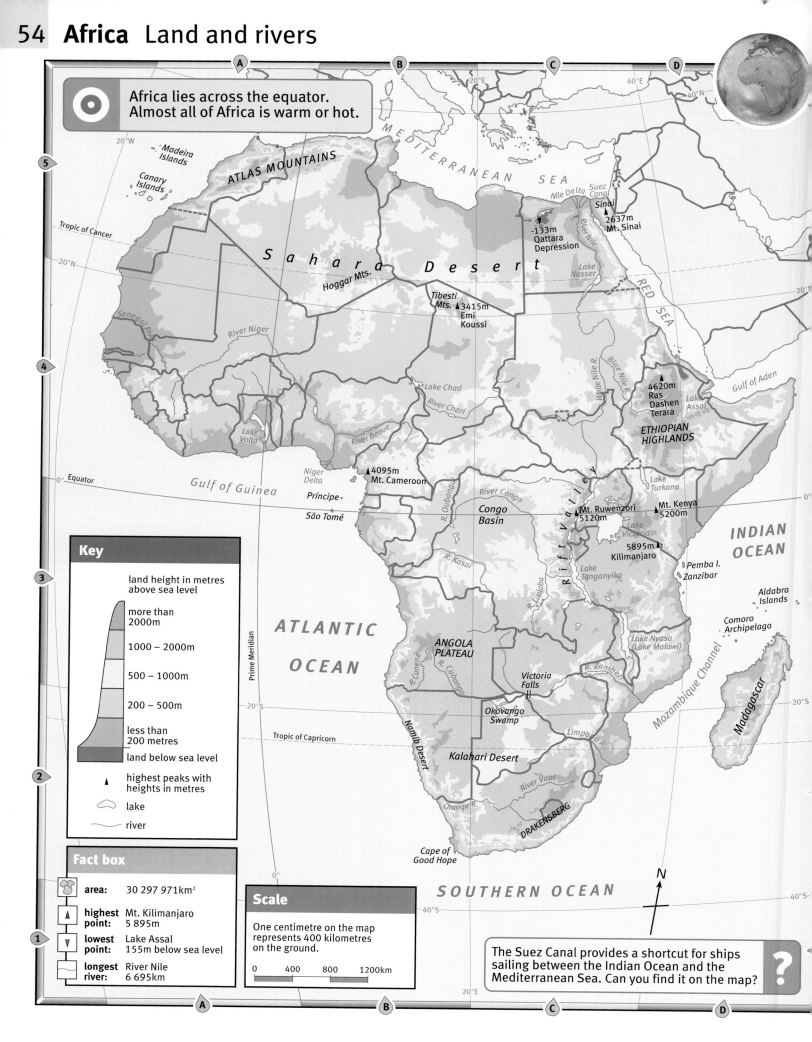

Africa lies across the equator.
Almost all of Africa is warm or hot.

A B C D

MEDITERRANEAN SEA

20°E 40°E 40°N

Madeira
Islands

ATLAS MOUNTAINS

Canary
Islands

20°W

Tropic of Cancer

20°N

S a h a r a   D e s e r t

Hoggar Mts.

Senegal Riv.

River Niger

Tibesti
Mts. ▲3415m
Emi
Koussi

Mile Delta

Suez
Canal

Sinai
▲2637m
Mt. Sinai

-133m
Qattara
Depression

Lake
Nasser

River Nile

RED SEA

20°

White Nile R.

Blue Nile R.

▲4620m
Ras
Dashen
Terara

Lake
Assal

Gulf of Aden

Lake Chad

River Chari

Lake
Volta

River Benue

ETHIOPIAN
HIGHLANDS

0° Equator

Gulf of Guinea

Niger
Delta

▲4095m
Mt. Cameroon

Príncipe

São Tomé

R. Oubangui

River Congo

Congo
Basin

R. Kasai

Rift Valley

Lake
Turkana

▲Mt. Ruwenzori
5120m

▲Mt. Kenya
5200m

Lake
Victoria

5895m▲
Kilimanjaro

INDIAN
OCEAN

0°

Pemba I.
Zanzibar

Lake
Tanganyika

Aldabra
Islands

Comoro
Archipelago

R. Lualaba

ATLANTIC

OCEAN

Prime Meridian

ANGOLA
PLATEAU

R. Cunene

R. Cubango

Lake Nyasa
(Lake Malawi)

Mozambique Channel

Madagascar

20°S

Victoria
Falls

R. Zambezi

Tropic of Capricorn

Namib Desert

Okovango
Swamp

Kalahari Desert

Limpopo R.

River Vaal

Orange R.

DRAKENSBERG

Cape of
Good Hope

0°

N

SOUTHERN OCEAN

40°S

20°E 40°

Key

land height in metres
above sea level

more than
2000m

1000 – 2000m

500 – 1000m

200 – 500m

less than
200 metres

land below sea level

▲ highest peaks with
heights in metres

lake

river

Fact box

🌍	**area:**	30 297 971km²
▲	**highest point**	Mt. Kilimanjaro 5 895m
▼	**lowest point**	Lake Assal 155m below sea level
	longest river:	River Nile 6 695km

Scale

One centimetre on the map
represents 400 kilometres
on the ground.

0   400   800   1200km

The Suez Canal provides a shortcut for ships
sailing between the Indian Ocean and the
Mediterranean Sea. Can you find it on the map?

?

Zenithal Equal Area Projection   © Oxford University Pre

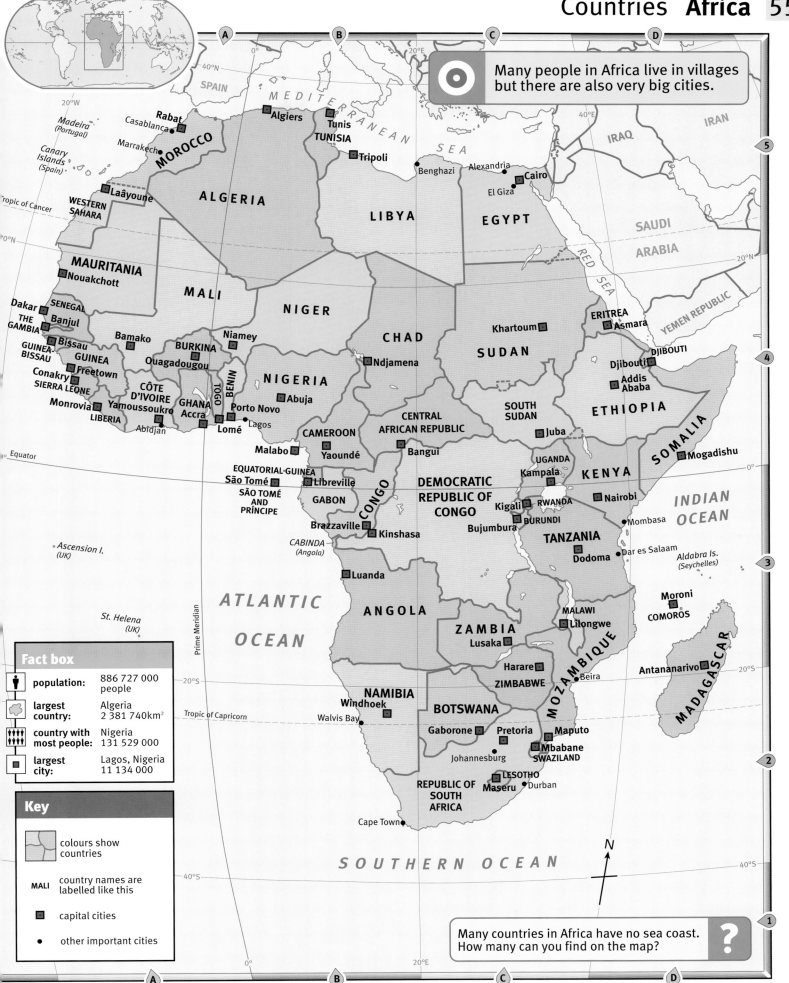

Many people in Africa live in villages but there are also very big cities.

SPAIN

MEDITERRANEAN SEA

Madeira
(Portugal)

Rabat
Casablanca
Marrakech
MOROCCO

Algiers
Tunis
TUNISIA
Tripoli

Benghazi
Alexandria
Cairo
El Giza

IRAQ
IRAN

Canary Islands
(Spain)

Laâyoune
WESTERN SAHARA

ALGERIA

LIBYA

EGYPT

SAUDI ARABIA

Tropic of Cancer

20°N

MAURITANIA
Nouakchott

MALI

NIGER

Khartoum

RED SEA

ERITREA
Asmara

YEMEN REPUBLIC

Dakar
SENEGAL
Banjul
THE GAMBIA
Bissau
GUINEA-BISSAU
Conakry
GUINEA
Freetown
SIERRA LEONE
Monrovia
LIBERIA

Bamako
BURKINA
Ouagadougou

Niamey

CHAD

SUDAN

Ndjamena

DJIBOUTI
Djibouti
Addis Ababa

NIGERIA
Abuja

CÔTE D'IVOIRE
Yamoussoukro
GHANA
Accra
TOGO
BENIN
Porto Novo
Lomé
Lagos
Abidjan

CAMEROON
Yaoundé
Malabo

CENTRAL AFRICAN REPUBLIC
Bangui

SOUTH SUDAN
Juba

ETHIOPIA

SOMALIA
Mogadishu

Equator

EQUATORIAL GUINEA
São Tomé
SÃO TOMÉ AND PRÍNCIPE
Libreville
GABON

CONGO
Brazzaville

DEMOCRATIC REPUBLIC OF CONGO
Kinshasa

UGANDA
Kampala
Kigali
RWANDA
Bujumbura
BURUNDI

KENYA
Nairobi
Mombasa

INDIAN OCEAN

CABINDA
(Angola)

Luanda

TANZANIA
Dodoma
Dar es Salaam

Aldabra Is.
(Seychelles)

Ascension I.
(UK)

ATLANTIC OCEAN

St. Helena
(UK)

ANGOLA

ZAMBIA
Lusaka

MALAWI
Lilongwe

Moroni
COMOROS

MADAGASCAR
Antananarivo

20°S

Harare
ZIMBABWE
Beira

MOZAMBIQUE

NAMIBIA
Windhoek

BOTSWANA

Walvis Bay

Gaborone
Pretoria
Maputo
Mbabane
SWAZILAND
Johannesburg

LESOTHO
Maseru
Durban

REPUBLIC OF SOUTH AFRICA

Cape Town

Tropic of Capricorn

SOUTHERN OCEAN

N

Prime Meridian

Fact box

👤	population:	886 727 000 people
🗺	largest country:	Algeria 2 381 740km²
👥	country with most people:	Nigeria 131 529 000
⬛	largest city:	Lagos, Nigeria 11 134 000

Key

colours show countries

MALI country names are labelled like this

⬛ capital cities

• other important cities

Many countries in Africa have no sea coast. How many can you find on the map?

?

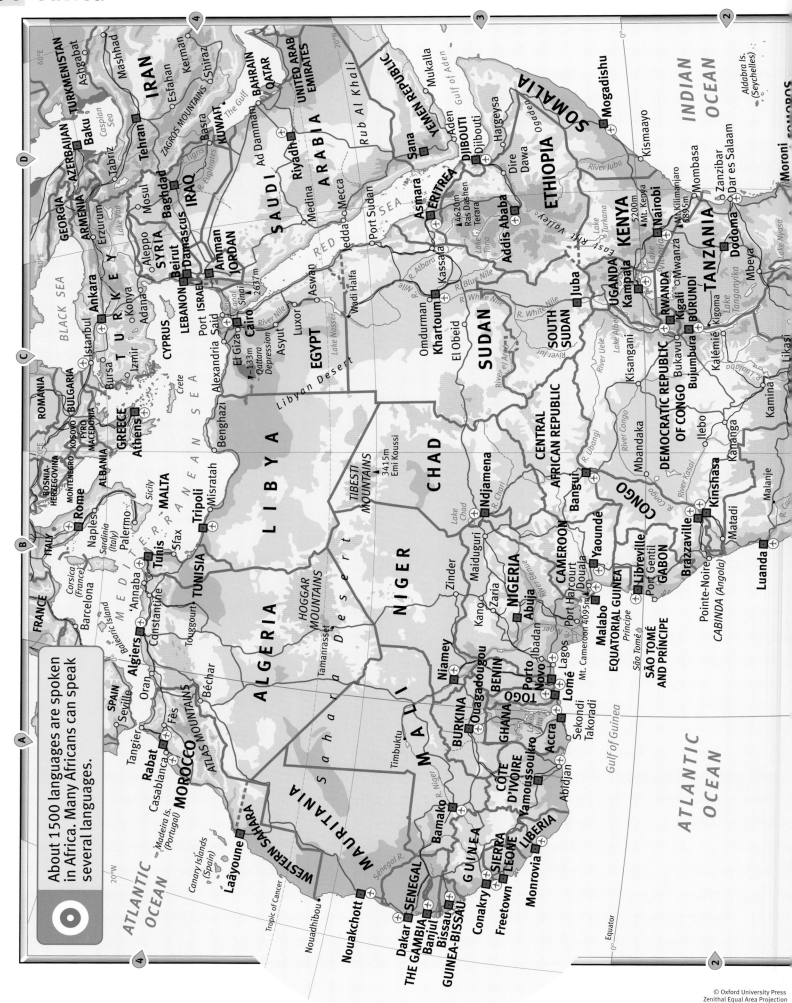

About 1500 languages are spoken in Africa. Many Africans can speak several languages.

© Oxford University Press
Zenithal Equal Area Projection

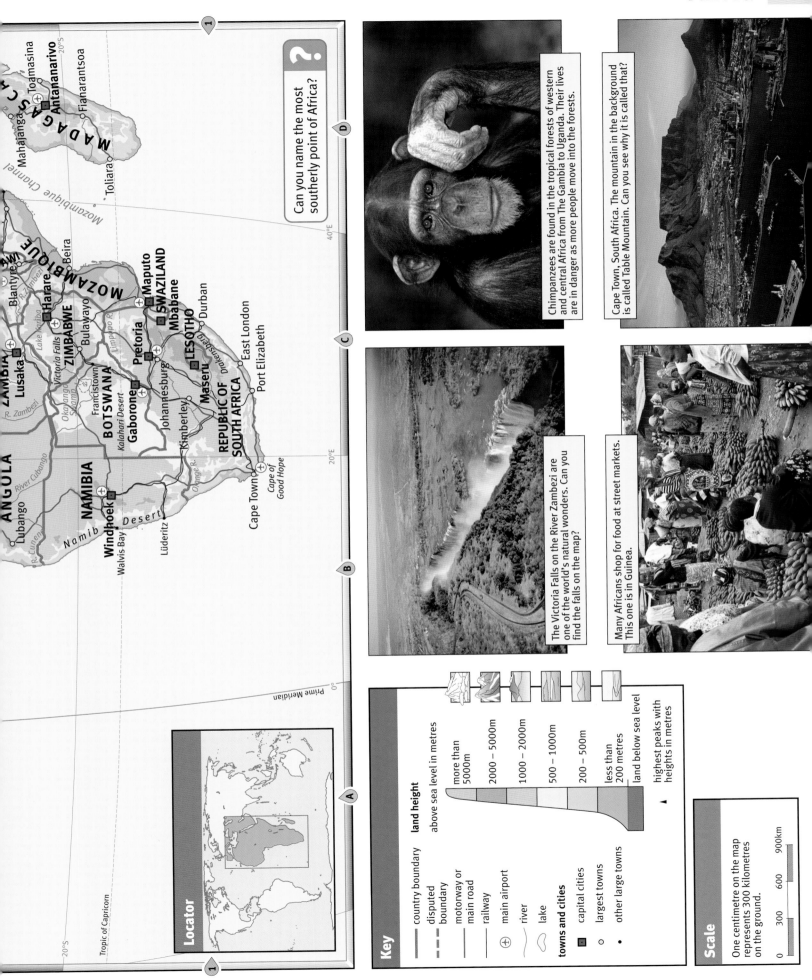

Map labels

MADAGASCAR
Mahajanga
Toamasina
Antananarivo
Fianarantsoa
Toliara
Mozambique Channel

MALAWI
Blantyre
Beira
Harare
ZIMBABWE
Bulawayo
Lake Kariba
R. Zambezi
Victoria Falls
ZAMBIA
Lusaka
MOZAMBIQUE
Maputo
SWAZILAND
Mbabane
Pretoria
LESOTHO
Maseru
Durban
Johannesburg
Kimberley
East London
Port Elizabeth
REPUBLIC OF SOUTH AFRICA
BOTSWANA
Gaborone
Francistown
Kalahari Desert
Limpopo R.
Drakensberg
Orange R.
Okavango Swamp
River Cubango
ANGOLA
Lubango
R. Cunene
NAMIBIA
Windhoek
Walvis Bay
Namib Desert
Lüderitz
Cape Town
Cape of Good Hope

20°S
Tropic of Capricorn
Prime Meridian
0°
20°E
40°E

Locator

Can you name the most southerly point of Africa?

Photo captions

Chimpanzees are found in the tropical forests of western and central Africa from The Gambia to Uganda. Their lives are in danger as more people move into the forests.

Cape Town, South Africa. The mountain in the background is called Table Mountain. Can you see why it is called that?

The Victoria Falls on the River Zambezi are one of the world's natural wonders. Can you find the falls on the map?

Many Africans shop for food at street markets. This one is in Guinea.

Key

land height
above sea level in metres

more than 5000m
2000 – 5000m
1000 – 2000m
500 – 1000m
200 – 500m
less than 200 metres
land below sea level

▲ highest peaks with heights in metres

country boundary
disputed boundary
motorway or main road
railway
⊕ main airport
river
lake

towns and cities
■ capital cities
○ largest towns
• other large towns

Scale

One centimetre on the map represents 300 kilometres on the ground.

0   300   600   900km

© Oxford University Press

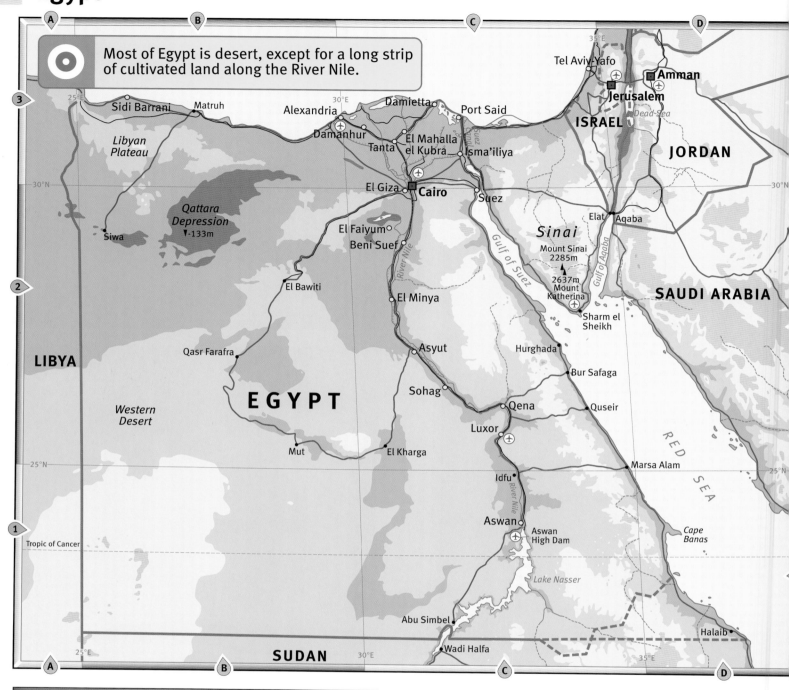

Most of Egypt is desert, except for a long strip of cultivated land along the River Nile.

A **B** **C** **D**

3

Sidi Barrani
Matruh
Alexandria
Damietta
Port Said
Tel Aviv-Yafo
Amman
Jerusalem
Dead Sea
ISRAEL
JORDAN
Damanhur
El Mahalla el Kubra
Tanta
Isma'iliya
Libyan Plateau

30°N

El Giza **Cairo**
Suez
Elat Aqaba
Sinai
Mount Sinai 2285m
2637m Mount Katherina

Qattara Depression ▼-133m
El Faiyum
Beni Suef
River Nile

Siwa

2

El Bawiti
El Minya
Gulf of Suez
Gulf of Aqaba
SAUDI ARABIA
Sharm el Sheikh

LIBYA

Qasr Farafra
Asyut
Hurghada
Bur Safaga

Western Desert
E G Y P T
Sohag
Qena
Quseir
RED SEA
Luxor
Mut
El Kharga

25°N

Idfu
Marsa Alam
Cape Banas

1

Tropic of Cancer
Aswan
Aswan High Dam
Lake Nasser

Abu Simbel
Halaib
Wadi Halfa

SUDAN

A **B** **C** **D**

25°E 30°E 35°E

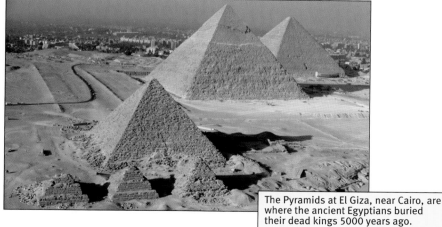

The Pyramids at El Giza, near Cairo, are where the ancient Egyptians buried their dead kings 5000 years ago.

The Aswan High Dam holds back the water of Lake Nasser and prevents the River Nile from flooding. Can you find the dam on the map? **?**

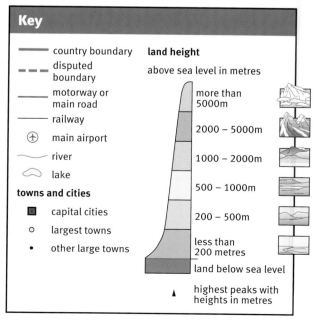

Key

— country boundary
--- disputed boundary
— motorway or main road
— railway
⊕ main airport
river
lake

towns and cities
■ capital cities
○ largest towns
• other large towns

land height

above sea level in metres

more than 5000m
2000 – 5000m
1000 – 2000m
500 – 1000m
200 – 500m
less than 200 metres
land below sea level

▲ highest peaks with heights in metres

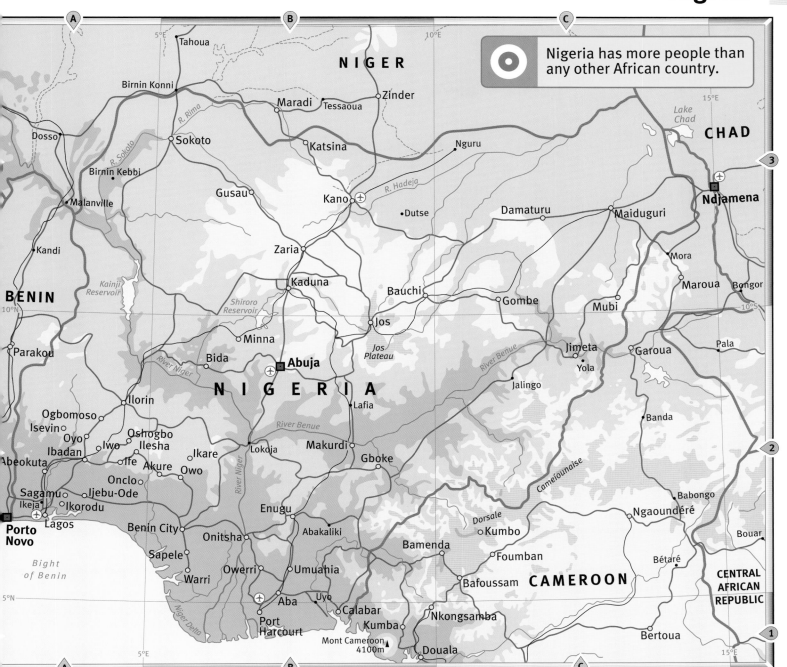

Nigeria has more people than any other African country.

NIGER

Tahoua
Birnin Konni
Maradi
Tessaoua
Zinder
R. Rima
Dosso
Sokoto
Katsina
Nguru
R. Sokoto
Birnin Kebbi
Malanville
Gusau
Kano
Dutse
Damaturu
Maiduguri
Ndjamena
CHAD
Lake Chad
R. Hadeja
Kandi
Zaria
Mora
Maroua
Bongor
BENIN
Kainji Reservoir
Kaduna
Bauchi
Gombe
Mubi
Shiroro Reservoir
Jos
Pala
Parakou
Minna
Jos Plateau
Jimeta
Garoua
Bida
Abuja
Yola
River Niger
NIGERIA
Jalingo
Banda
Ilorin
Lafia
River Benue
Ogbomoso
Isevin
Oyo
Oshogbo
Ilesha
Ikare
Lokoja
Makurdi
River Benue
Iwo
Ibadan
Ife
Akure
Owo
Gboke
Cameltounaise
Abeokuta
Onclo
Ijebu-Ode
River Niger
Babongo
Sagamu
Ikeja
Ikorodu
Enugu
Ngaoundéré
Bouar
Porto Novo
Lagos
Benin City
Onitsha
Abakaliki
Dorsale
Kumbo
Bight of Benin
Sapele
Owerri
Umuahia
Bamenda
Foumban
Bétaré
CENTRAL AFRICAN REPUBLIC
Warri
Aba
Uyo
Bafoussam
CAMEROON
Niger Delta
Port Harcourt
Calabar
Kumba
Nkongsamba
Bertoua
Mont Cameroon 4100m
Douala

Scale

One centimetre on the map represents 70 kilometres on the ground.

0 70 140 210km

Locator

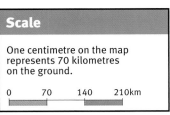

Nigeria   Egypt

Two thirds of Nigerians live in farming villages.

Abuja is the capital of Nigeria but Lagos is the largest city. Can you find Lagos on the map?

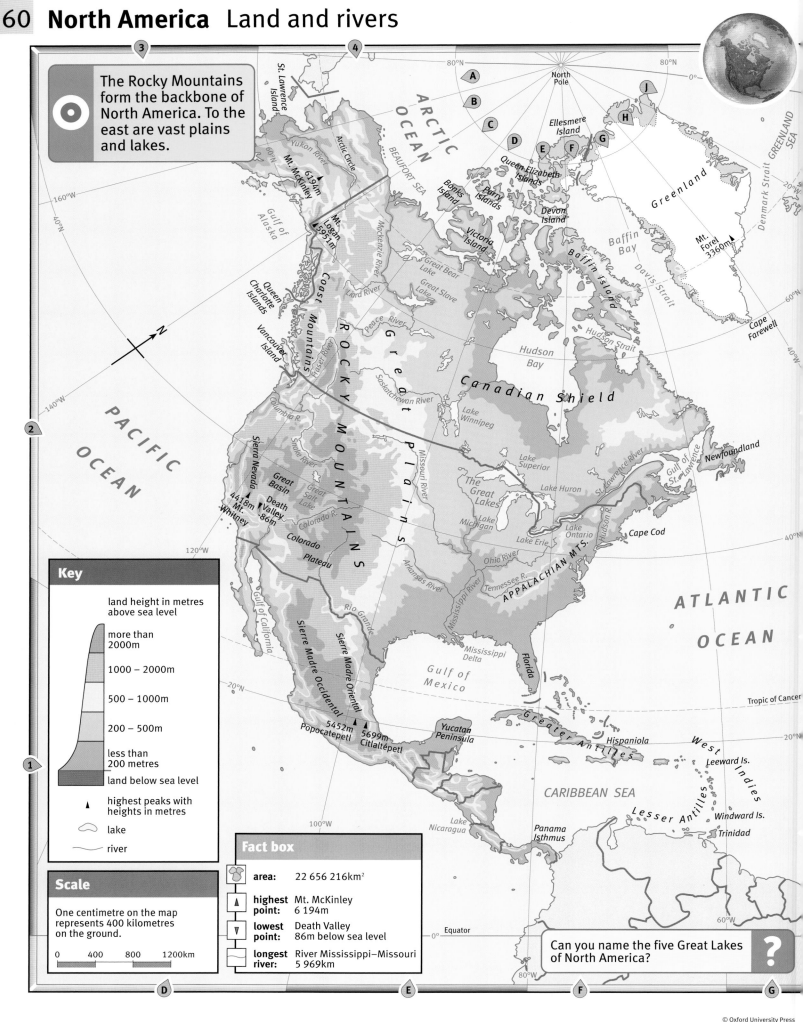

⊙ The Rocky Mountains form the backbone of North America. To the east are vast plains and lakes.

Key

land height in metres above sea level

- more than 2000m
- 1000 – 2000m
- 500 – 1000m
- 200 – 500m
- less than 200 metres
- land below sea level

▲ highest peaks with heights in metres

lake

river

Scale

One centimetre on the map represents 400 kilometres on the ground.

0   400   800   1200km

Fact box

	area:	22 656 216km²
▲	**highest point:**	Mt. McKinley 6 194m
▼	**lowest point:**	Death Valley 86m below sea level
	longest river:	River Mississippi–Missouri 5 969km

? Can you name the five Great Lakes of North America?

ARCTIC OCEAN

BEAUFORT SEA

PACIFIC OCEAN

ATLANTIC OCEAN

CARIBBEAN SEA

Gulf of Mexico

Greenland

Mt. Forel 3360m

Denmark Strait
GREENLAND SEA
Davis Strait
Baffin Bay
Cape Farewell
Hudson Strait
Baffin Island
Ellesmere Island
Queen Elizabeth Islands
Devon Island
Parry Islands
Banks Island
Victoria Island
Great Bear Lake
Great Slave Lake
Hudson Bay
Canadian Shield

North Pole

St. Lawrence Island
Arctic Circle
Yukon River
Mt. McKinley 6194m
Mt. Logan 5951m
Gulf of Alaska
Queen Charlotte Islands
Vancouver Island
Coast Mountains
Mackenzie River
Liard River
Peace River
Fraser River
Columbia R.
Snake River
Saskatchewan River
Great Plains
Missouri River
ROCKY MOUNTAINS

Lake Winnipeg
Lake Superior
Lake Huron
Lake Michigan
The Great Lakes
Lake Erie
Lake Ontario
St. Lawrence River
Gulf of St. Lawrence
Newfoundland
Hudson R.
Cape Cod

Sierra Nevada
Great Basin
Great Salt Lake
4418m Mt. Whitney
Death Valley -86m
Colorado R.
Colorado Plateau
APPALACHIAN MTS.
Ohio River
Tennessee R.
Arkansas River
Mississippi River
Rio Grande
Gulf of California
Sierra Madre Occidental
Sierra Madre Oriental
5452m Popocatepetl
5699m Citlaltépetl
Mississippi Delta
Florida
Yucatan Peninsula
Greater Antilles
Hispaniola
Leeward Is.
West Indies
Lesser Antilles
Windward Is.
Trinidad
Lake Nicaragua
Panama Isthmus

Tropic of Cancer
Equator

80°N 80°N
0°
20°W
40°N 40°N 40°N
60°N
60°N
20°N 20°N
160°W
140°W
120°W
100°W
80°W
60°W
0°

A B C D E F G H J

© Oxford University Press
Oblique Mercator Projection

4 80°N 60°N

A
B
C
D E F G

ARCTIC OCEAN

The large countries of Canada, the United States and Mexico make up most of North America.

4

GREENLAND (Denmark)

160°W

USA
ALASKA

Anchorage

20°W

60°N

Nuuk

Arctic Circle

C A N A D A

Vancouver
Edmonton
Seattle
Calgary
Portland

3

40°W

Winnipeg

PACIFIC

OCEAN

N

San Francisco
Sacremento
Salt Lake City
Minneapolis
Québec
Ottawa
Montréal
Halifax

St-Pierre & Miquelon (France)

140°W

Los Angeles
San Diego
Denver
Chicago
Detroit
Toronto
Boston
New York

UNITED STATES OF AMERICA

Kansas City
Pittsburgh
Washington D.C.
Philadelphia

40°N

Tropic of Cancer

Phoenix
St Louis

ATLANTIC

20°N

120°W

Dallas
Atlanta

Bermuda (UK)

OCEAN

2

Houston

Monterrey
New Orleans

Gulf of Mexico

Miami

THE BAHAMAS
Nassau

Fact box

👤	population:	511 166 000 people
🗺	largest country:	Canada 9 970 601km²
👥	country with most people:	USA 298 213 000
◼	largest city:	Mexico City, Mexico 18 934 000

Guadalajara

MEXICO

Mexico City

Puebla

Havana

C U B A

DOMINICAN REPUBLIC

PUERTO RICO (USA)

20°N

Belmopan
Kingston
Santo Domingo
San Juan

ST. KITTS AND NEVIS
ANTIGUA & BARBUDA
DOMINICA

GUATEMALA
BELIZE
HONDURAS
Guatemala City
San Salvador
EL SALVADOR
NICARAGUA
Tegucigalpa
Managua

JAMAICA
HAITI
Port-au-Prince

CARIBBEAN SEA

ST. VINCENT & THE GRENADINES
ST. LUCIA
BARBADOS
GRENADA

Key

▦	colours show countries
CUBA	country names are labelled like this
◼	capital cities
•	other important cities

San José
COSTA RICA

Panama City
PANAMA

Port of Spain
TRINIDAD & TOBAGO

1

VENEZUELA

GUYANA

COLOMBIA

80°W

60°W

Equator 0°

100°W

The capital of the USA is **Washington D.C.** Can you find out what **D.C.** stands for?

?

D E F G

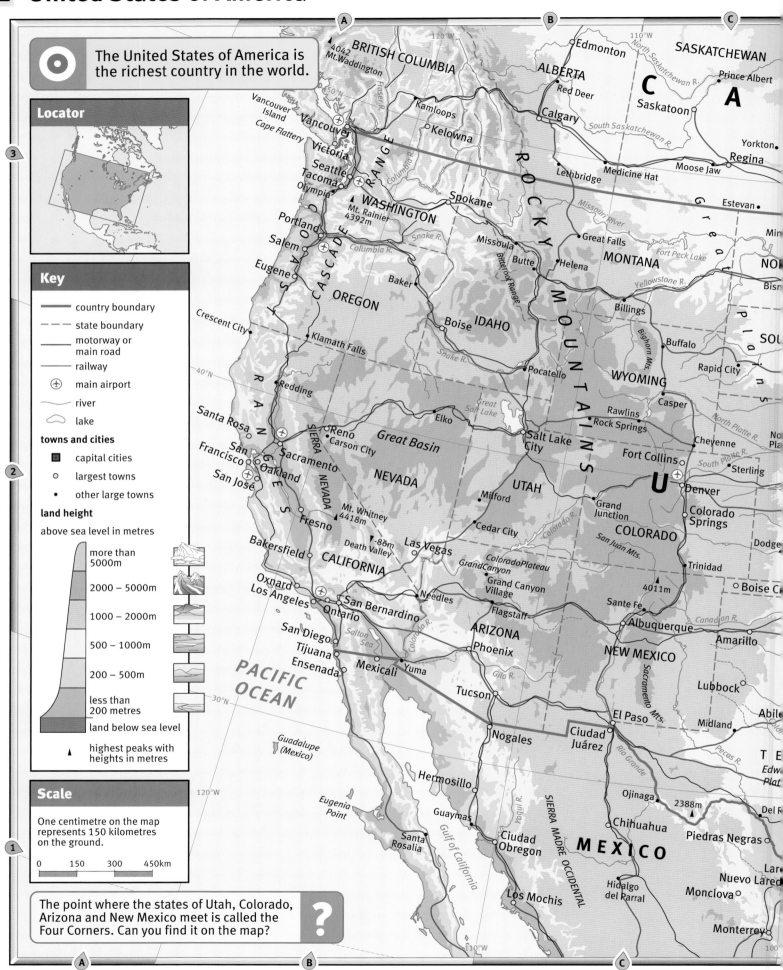

The United States of America is the richest country in the world.

Locator

Key

— country boundary
-- state boundary
— motorway or main road
— railway
⊕ main airport
river
lake

towns and cities
■ capital cities
○ largest towns
• other large towns

land height
above sea level in metres

more than 5000m
2000 – 5000m
1000 – 2000m
500 – 1000m
200 – 500m
less than 200 metres
land below sea level
▲ highest peaks with heights in metres

Scale

One centimetre on the map represents 150 kilometres on the ground.

0   150   300   450km

The point where the states of Utah, Colorado, Arizona and New Mexico meet is called the Four Corners. Can you find it on the map?

?

BRITISH COLUMBIA
▲4042 Mt.Waddington
150°N
Vancouver Island
Cape Flattery
Vancouver
Victoria
Seattle
Tacoma
Olympia
WASHINGTON
▲ Mt. Rainier 4392m
Kamloops
Kelowna
Spokane
Portland
Salem
Eugene
CASCADE RANGE
Columbia R.
Snake R.
OREGON
Crescent City
Klamath Falls
40°N
Redding
Santa Rosa
Reno
Carson City
San Francisco
Oakland
Sacramento
San José
SIERRA NEVADA
Fresno
Great Basin
Elko
NEVADA
Mt. Whitney ▲4418m
Bakersfield
Death Valley -86m
Las Vegas
CALIFORNIA
Oxnard
Los Angeles
Ontario
San Bernardino
Needles
San Diego
Tijuana
Ensenada
Mexicali
Yuma
Salton Sea
Gila R.
Colorado R.
ARIZONA
Phoenix
Tucson
PACIFIC OCEAN
30°N
120°W
Guadalupe (Mexico)
Eugenia Point
Santa Rosalía
Guaymas
Gulf of California
Nogales
Hermosillo
Ciudad Obregon
Los Mochis

Edmonton
ALBERTA
Red Deer
Calgary
Lethbridge
Medicine Hat
SASKATCHEWAN
North Saskatchewan R.
Prince Albert
Saskatoon
South Saskatchewan R.
Yorkton
Regina
Moose Jaw
Estevan
C A N A D A
Missouri River
Great Falls
Fort Peck Lake
MONTANA
Missoula
Butte
Helena
Baker
Boise
IDAHO
Snake R.
Pocatello
Great Salt Lake
Salt Lake City
UTAH
Milford
Cedar City
Colorado R.
Grand Junction
Grand Canyon
ColoradoPlateau
GrandCanyon Village
Flagstaff
San Juan Mts.
▲4011m
Sante Fe
Albuquerque
NEW MEXICO
Sacramento Mts.
El Paso
Ciudad Juárez
Nogales
Ojinaga
2388m ▲
Chihuahua
Hidalgo del Parral
M E X I C O
SIERRA MADRE OCCIDENTAL
Rio Grande
ROCKY MOUNTAINS
Bitterroot Range
Yellowstone R.
Billings
Bighorn Mts.
Buffalo
WYOMING
Rapid City
Rawlins
Rock Springs
Casper
North Platte R.
Cheyenne
Fort Collins
South Platte R.
Sterling
U
Denver
COLORADO
Colorado Springs
Trinidad
Dodge
Amarillo
Lubbock
Midland
Abile
Edwa Plat
Del R
Piedras Negras
Monclova
Nuevo Lare
Monterrey
Laredo
Pecos R.
Canadian R.
Great Plains
NO
SOU
Bisn
Min
Boise C
TE
Spokane
120°W
110°W

© Oxford University Press
Conical Orthomorphic Projection

110°W

D 90°W E 80°W F 70°W G 4 50°N

CANADA

QUÉBEC

Norway House
Lake Winnipeg
Akimiski Island
James Bay
Attawapiskat
Moosonee
Waskaganish
Lac Mistassini
Sept-Îles
Île d'Anticosti
Gaspé

MANITOBA
ONTARIO
Réservoir Gouin
Saquenay
Rivière-du-Loup
Baie Comeau
NEW BRUNSWICK

Lake Manitoba
Portage La Prairie
Brandon
Winnipeg
Lake of the Woods
Hearst
Cochrane
Rouyn-Noranda
Val-d'Or
Québec
Sherbrooke
Presque Isle
Fredericton
Saint John
Bay of Fundy

Longlac
Lake Nipigon
Timmins
MAINE
Bangor
Augusta
Yarmouth

Thunder Bay
Upper Red Lake
Michipicoten
The Great Lakes
Sudbury
North Bay
Montréal
St. Lawrence
Portland

Grand Forks
Bemidji
Lower Red Lake
Marquette
Sault Ste. Marie
Ottawa
Kingston
NEW YORK
VERMONT
NEW HAMPSHIRE
Concord
Boston
Cape Cod

KOTA
Fargo
MINNESOTA
Duluth
Ironwood
Lake Superior
WISCONSIN
Lake Huron
Toronto
Lake Ontario
Rochester
Syracuse
Albany
MASSACHUSETTS
CONNECTICUT
RHODE ISLAND
Providence
Hartford

Minneapolis
St. Paul
Green Bay
Traverse City
MICHIGAN
Lake Michigan
St. Catharines
Buffalo
Scranton
New York

Mitchell
Albert Lea
Madison
Grand Rapids
Lansing
Detroit
Lake Erie
Cleveland
PENNSYLVANIA
Newark
Trenton
Philadelphia
NEW JERSEY

Sioux Falls
Sioux City
IOWA
Cedar Rapids
Milwaukee
Chicago
Fort Wayne
Toledo
Akron
Pittsburgh
Harrisburg
Dover
DELAWARE
MARYLAND

Des Moines
Iowa City
ILLINOIS
Bloomington
INDIANA
OHIO
Columbus
Baltimore
Washington D.C.

Omaha
Lincoln
Springfield
Indianapolis
Cincinnati
WEST VIRGINIA
Charleston
Richmond
Chesapeake Bay

U S A

NEBRASKA
Topeka
Salina
Kansas City
Jefferson City
St. Louis
Louisville
Frankfort
Lexington
Ohio R.
VIRGINIA
Norfolk

KANSAS
Wichita
MISSOURI
Springfield
Ozark Plateau
KENTUCKY
Bowling Green
APPALACHIAN MTS.
Greensboro
Raleigh
Cape Hatteras

Missouri R.
Nashville
Tennessee R.
Knoxville
Charlotte
NORTH CAROLINA

ATLANTIC OCEAN

Oklahoma City
Tulsa
Fort Smith
White R.
TENNESSEE
Chattanooga
Greenville
Wilmington

OKLAHOMA
Little Rock
Arkansas R.
Memphis
Florence
SOUTH CAROLINA
Columbia
Charleston

Wichita Falls
Red River
ARKANSAS
Birmingham
Atlanta
GEORGIA
Macon
Savannah R.

Fort Worth
Dallas
Texarkana
MISSISSIPPI
Meridian
ALABAMA
Columbus
Savannah

Shreveport
Jackson
Montgomery
Alabama R.

Brazos R.
Huntsville
LOUISIANA
Baton Rouge
Mobile
Jacksonville
30°N

Austin
Houston
Lafayette
New Orleans
Tallahassee
Daytona Beach

San Antonio
Galveston
Mississippi Delta
Orlando
Cape Canaveral

Corpus Christi
Gulf of Mexico
Tampa
St. Petersburg
FLORIDA
Lake Okeechobee
West Palm Beach
Freeport
Grand Bahama
Great Abaco
THE BAHAMAS

Reynosa
Matamoros
Rio Grande
Naples
Miami
Florida Keys
Straits of Florida
Nassau
New Providence Island
Eleuthera
Cat Island
Andros
Tropic of Cancer
Long Island

The Rocky Mountains stretch over 1000 miles. Find them on the map.

© Oxford University Press

The chain of islands that enclose the Caribbean Sea is called the West Indies.

Chichen Itza is a pyramid in the Yucatan Peninsula built by the Maya people before Columbus sailed to the Americas.

The climate and scenery of the Caribbean make it a popular tourist destination.

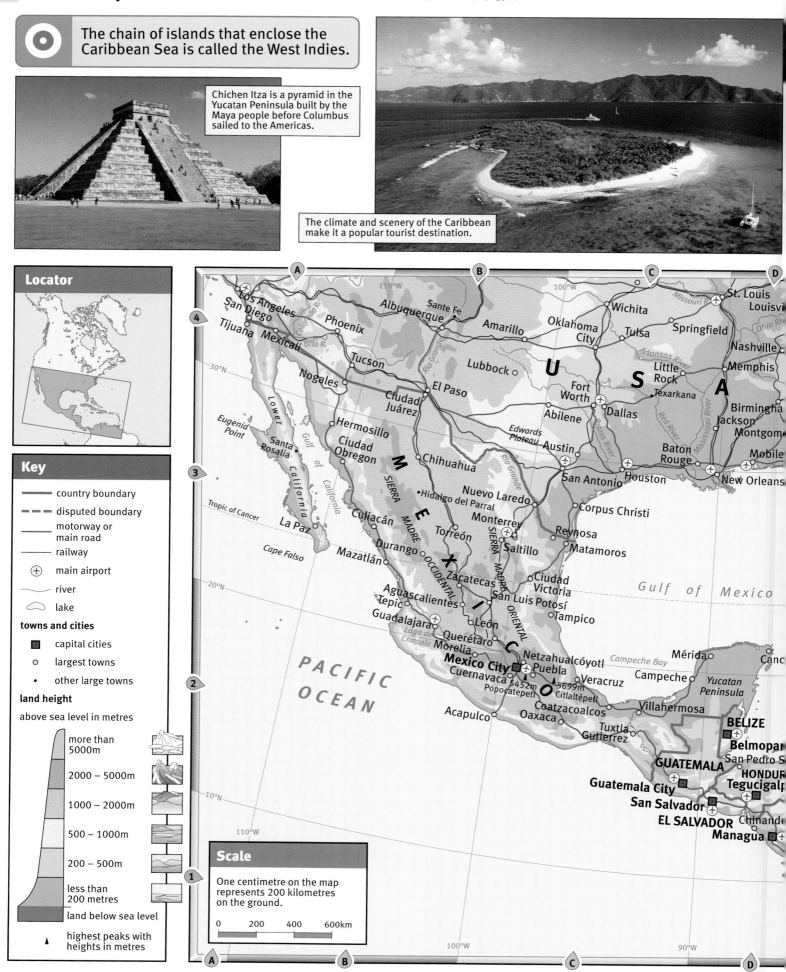

Locator

Key

———	country boundary
---	disputed boundary
———	motorway or main road
—	railway
⊕	main airport
∿	river
⬡	lake

towns and cities

▣	capital cities
○	largest towns
•	other large towns

land height

above sea level in metres

- more than 5000m
- 2000 – 5000m
- 1000 – 2000m
- 500 – 1000m
- 200 – 500m
- less than 200 metres
- land below sea level
- ▲ highest peaks with heights in metres

Scale

One centimetre on the map represents 200 kilometres on the ground.

0   200   400   600km

Map labels:

110°W 100°W 90°W 100°W
30°N 20°N 10°N

Los Angeles, San Diego, Tijuana, Mexicali, Phoenix, Tucson, Nogales, Albuquerque, Sante Fe, Amarillo, Oklahoma City, Wichita, Tulsa, Springfield, St. Louis, Louisvi, Nashville, Memphis, Little Rock, Texarkana, Birmingha, Jackson, Montgom, Mobile, Lubbock, Fort Worth, Abilene, Dallas, Baton Rouge, New Orleans

U S A

Colorado R., Gila R., Rio Grande, Edwards Plateau, Arkansas River, Red River, Brazos River, Mississippi River, Ohio Riv., Missouri R.

Ciudad Juárez, El Paso, Hermosillo, Ciudad Obregon, Chihuahua, •Hidalgo del Parral, Nuevo Laredo, Monterrey, San Antonio, Corpus Christi, Reynosa, Matamoros, Houston

Eugenia Point, Santa Rosalia, La Paz, Cape Falso, Lower California, Gulf of California

Tropic of Cancer

M E X I C O

SIERRA MADRE OCCIDENTAL, SIERRA MADRE ORIENTAL

Culiacán, Torreón, Durango, Mazatlán, Zacatecas, Saltillo, Ciudad Victoria, San Luis Potosí, Tampico, Aguascalientes, Tepic, León, Guadalajara, Querétaro, Morelia, Lago de Chapala, Netzahualcóyotl, Mexico City, Puebla, Cuernavaca, 5452m Popocatepetl, 5699m Citlaltépetl, Veracruz, Campeche Bay, Mérida, Canc, Campeche, Yucatan Peninsula, Villahermosa, Coatzacoalcos, Oaxaca, Acapulco, Tuxtla Gutierrez

Gulf of Mexico

PACIFIC OCEAN

BELIZE, Belmopan, San Pedro S, GUATEMALA, Guatemala City, HONDUR, Tegucigalp, San Salvador, EL SALVADOR, Chinande, Managua

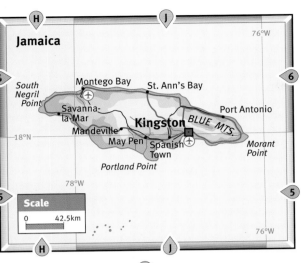

Jamaica

South Negril Point
Montego Bay
St. Ann's Bay
Savanna-la-Mar
Mandeville
Kingston
BLUE MTS.
Port Antonio
May Pen
Spanish Town
Morant Point
Portland Point

76°W
18°N
78°W
76°W

H J

Scale
0 42.5km

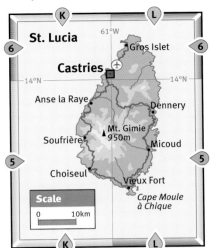

St. Lucia

Gros Islet
Castries
Anse la Raye
Dennery
14°N
Soufrière
▲ Mt. Gimie 950m
Micoud
Choiseul
Vieux Fort
Cape Moule à Chique

61°W
14°N

K L

Scale
0 10km

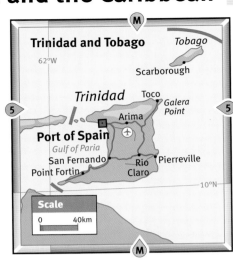

Trinidad and Tobago

Tobago
Scarborough
Trinidad
Toco
Galera Point
Arima
Port of Spain
Gulf of Paria
San Fernando
Rio Claro
Pierreville
Point Fortin

62°W
10°N

M

Scale
0 40km

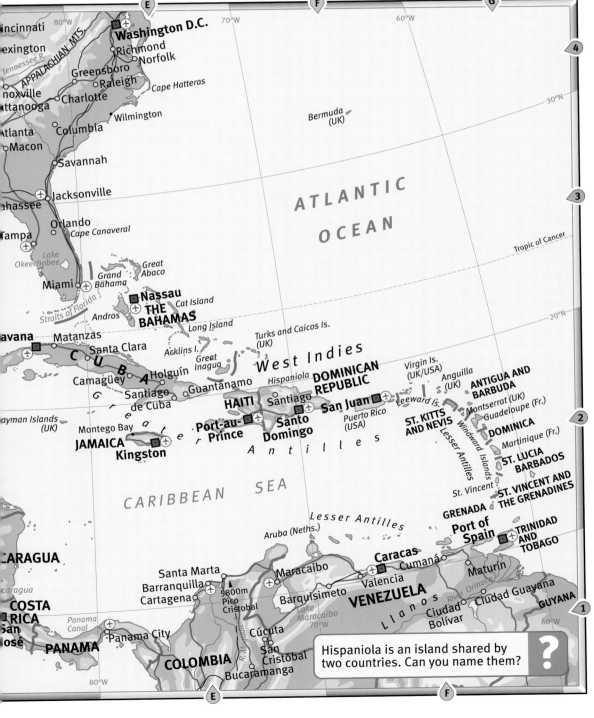

Cincinnati
Lexington
80°W
Washington D.C.
Richmond
Norfolk
APPALACHIAN MTS.
Tennessee R.
Greensboro
Knoxville
Raleigh
Chattanooga
Charlotte
Cape Hatteras
Atlanta
Columbia
Macon
Wilmington
Savannah
Tallahassee
Jacksonville
Orlando
Tampa
Cape Canaveral
Lake Okeechobee
Miami
Grand Bahama
Great Abaco
Straits of Florida
Nassau
THE BAHAMAS
Cat Island
Andros
Long Island
Havana
Matanzas
Santa Clara
C U B A
Holguín
Camagüey
Santiago de Cuba
Guantánamo
Acklins I.
Great Inagua
Turks and Caicos Is. (UK)
West Indies
Hispaniola
DOMINICAN REPUBLIC
HAITI
Santiago
San Juan
Virgin Is. (UK/USA)
Anguilla (UK)
ANTIGUA AND BARBUDA
Montserrat (UK)
Guadeloupe (Fr.)
Cayman Islands (UK)
Montego Bay
JAMAICA
Kingston
Port-au-Prince
Santo Domingo
Puerto Rico (USA)
Leeward Is.
ST. KITTS AND NEVIS
DOMINICA
Martinique (Fr.)
G r e a t e r   A n t i l l e s
Windward Islands
Lesser Antilles
ST. LUCIA
BARBADOS
CARIBBEAN SEA
St. Vincent
ST. VINCENT AND THE GRENADINES
Lesser Antilles
GRENADA
Aruba (Neths.)
Port of Spain
TRINIDAD AND TOBAGO
NICARAGUA
COSTA RICA
San José
Santa Marta
Barranquilla
Cartagena
Caracas
Cumaná
Maracaibo
Valencia
Maturín
5800m Pico Cristobal
Barquisimeto
VENEZUELA
Ciudad Guayana
Panama Canal
Panama City
PANAMA
Lake Maracaibo
Llanos
Ciudad Bolívar
River Orinoco
GUYANA
COLOMBIA
Cúcuta
San Cristóbal
Bucaramanga
R. Magdalena

ATLANTIC OCEAN

Bermuda (UK)

30°N
Tropic of Cancer
20°N
70°W
60°W
80°W
70°W
60°W

E F G
4
3
2
1

Hispaniola is an island shared by two countries. Can you name them? **?**

The Panama Canal allows ships to sail between the Caribbean Sea and the Pacific Ocean. Can you find it on the map?

The keel-billed toucan is the national bird of Belize.

The Andes are the longest mountain range in the world and stretch the whole length of South America.

Key

land height in metres above sea level

more than 2000m

1000 – 2000m

500 – 1000m

200 – 500m

less than 200 metres

land below sea level

▲ highest peaks with heights in metres

⌒ lake

〜 river

Fact box

area: 17 867 239km²

highest point: Aconcagua 6 960m

lowest point: Valdés Peninsula 40m below sea level

longest river: River Amazon 6 516km

Scale

One centimetre on the map represents 350 kilometres on the ground.

0   350   700   850km

Can you find out which famous scientist studied plants and animals on the Galapagos Islands in 1835?

PACIFIC OCEAN

ATLANTIC OCEAN

ATLANTIC OCEAN

SOUTHERN OCEAN

Cocos Islands

Galapagos Islands

Equator

Cotopaxi 5896m
Chimborazo 6310m

Lake Maracaibo

L l a n o s

River Orinoco

GUIANA HIGHLANDS

Mt. Roraima ▲2810m

River Negro

River Amazon

River Amazon

Amazon Basin

S e l v a s

River Madeira

River Topajos

River Tocantins

River São Francisco

Rocas Island

Mato Grosso

BRAZILIAN HIGHLANDS

River Magdalena

River Ucayali

A N D E S

Lake Titicaca

Lake Poopo

Atacama Desert

River Pilcomayo

River Paraguay

G r a n C h a c o

River Paraná

River Uruguay

P a m p a s

Río de la Plata

6908m Ojos del Salado

Aconcagua 6960m

Juan Fernández Islands

R. Colorado

R. Negro

Patagonia

Chiloé Island

Valdés Peninsula

Falkland Islands

Tierra del Fuego

Cape Horn

South Georgia

Tropic of Capricorn

N

© Oxford University Press
Oblique Mercator Projection

CARIBBEAN SEA

Brazilians speak Portuguese. Most other South Americans speak Spanish.

COSTA RICA

PANAMA

Barranquilla
Maracaibo
Caracas
Valencia
VENEZUELA
Medellin
Georgetown
GUYANA
Paramaribo
SURINAME
Cayenne
French Guiana (France)
Cali
Bogota
COLOMBIA

ATLANTIC OCEAN

Equator

Quito
ECUADOR
Guayaquil

Galapagos Islands (Ecuador)

Belem

Iquitos

Manaus

Rocas Island (Brazil)

Fortaleza

Trujillo
PERU

B R A Z I L

Recife

Lima

Salvador

Arequipa
BOLIVIA
La Paz
Santa Cruz
Sucre

Brásília

Belo Horizonte

PACIFIC OCEAN

PARAGUAY

Antofagasta

Rio de Janeiro
São Paulo
Curitiba

Asunción

opic of Capricorn

C H I L E

Porto Alegre

Cordoba
Rosario

URUGUAY
Santiago
Juan Fernandez Is. (Chile)
Buenos Aires
Montevideo

ATLANTIC OCEAN

ARGENTINA
Mar del Plata

Concepcion

N

Fact box

population:	370 056 000 people	
largest country:	Brazil 8 547 361km²	
country with most people:	Brazil 186 405 000	
largest city:	São Paulo 19 591 000	

Stanley
Falkland Islands (UK)

South Georgia (UK)

Punta Arenas

SOUTHERN OCEAN

Key

colours show countries

PERU country names are labelled like this

■ capital cities

• other important cities

South America contains the world's longest, thinnest country. Can you name it? **?**

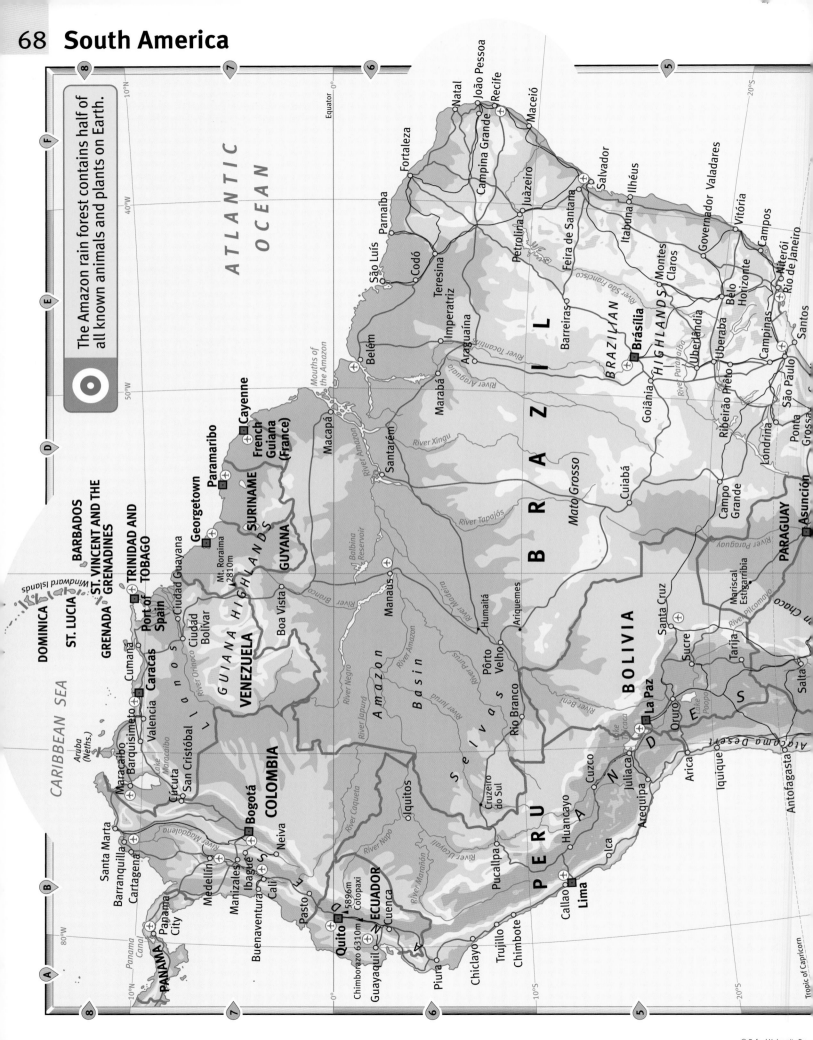

Key

- country boundary
- disputed boundary
- motorway or main road
- railway
- ⊕ main airport
- river
- lake

towns and cities
- ■ capital cities
- ○ largest towns
- • other large towns

land height

above sea level in metres
- more than 5000m
- 2000 – 5000m
- 1000 – 2000m
- 500 – 1000m
- 200 – 500m
- less than 200 metres
- land below sea level
- ▲ highest peaks with heights in metres

Scale

One centimetre on the map represents 210 kilometres on the ground.

0   210   420   630km

Locator

The capital of Brazil was built as a brand new city in 1960. Can you name it?

Colourful houses in the La Boca neighbourhood of Buenos Aires, Argentina.

Uros people of Lake Titicaca, Peru and Bolivia, waiting for tourists to arrive on their floating island made from bundles of reeds.

The Sugar Loaf Mountain, Rio de Janeiro. Can you find Rio on the map?

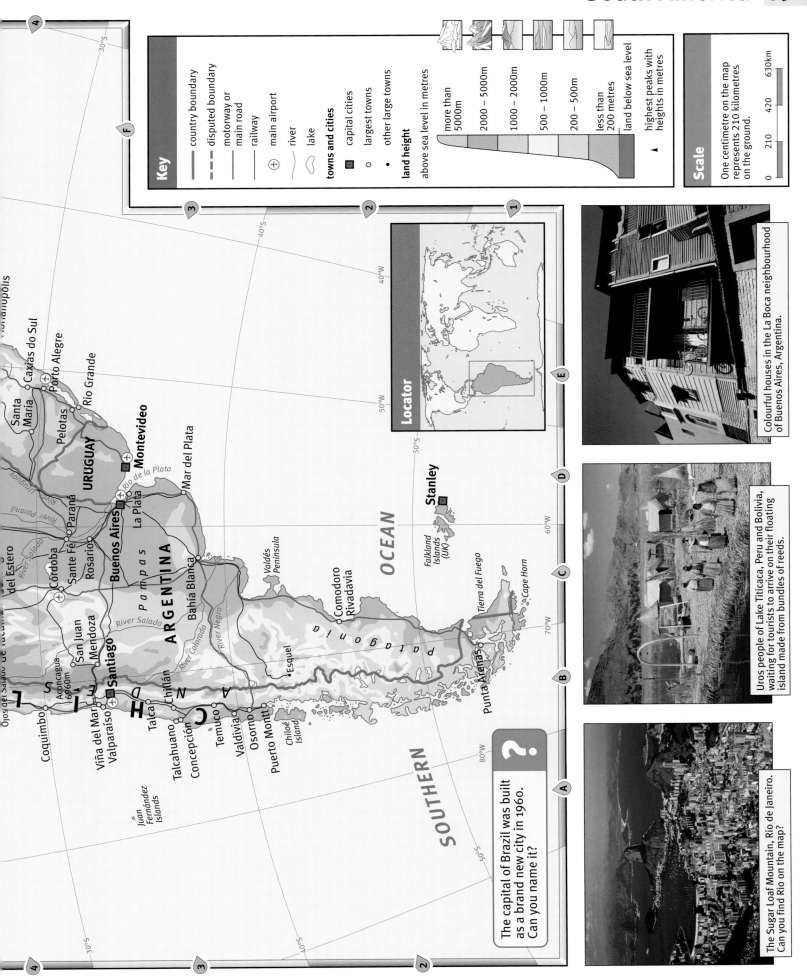

Australia is by far the largest country in Oceania. The rest of Oceania is made up of many groups of islands.

Key

land height in metres above sea level

more than 2000m

1000 – 2000m

500 – 1000m

200 – 500m

less than 200 metres

land below sea level

▲ highest peaks with heights in metres

lake

river

Scale

One centimetre on the map represents 450 kilometres on the ground.

0   450   900   1350km

Map 1 (Land and rivers)

Equator

120°E   140°E   160°E

BISMARCK SEA

New Guinea

5030m ▲ Pk. Jaya

4905m ▼ Mt. Wilhelm

ARAFURA SEA

Solomon Islands

TIMOR SEA

CORAL SEA

Cape York Peninsula

Arnhem Land

Gulf of Carpentaria

Espiritu Santo

INDIAN OCEAN

Kimberley Plateau

R. Fitzroy

Great Barrier Reef

Great Dividing Range

R. Flinders

New Caledonia (Fr.)

20°S

Great Sandy Desert

Hamersley Range 1235m
Mt. Tom Price

Gibson Desert

Macdonnell Ranges

▲ Ayers Rock 867m

Simpson Desert

Lake Eyre

Tropic of Capricorn

PACIFIC OCEAN

Norfolk I. (Aust.)

Lord Howe I. (Aust.)

Great Victoria Desert

L. Torrens   R. Darling

Nullarbor Plain

Great Australian Bight

R. Murray

Great Dividing Range

▲ 2230m Mt. Kosciusko

TASMAN SEA

North Island

C. Leeuwin

N

3764m Mt. Cook
Southern Alps
South Island

Bass Strait

Tasmania

SOUTHERN OCEAN

40°S

120°E   140°E   160°E   180°

Map 2 (Countries)

Equator   120°E   140°E

INDONESIA

EAST TIMOR

PAPUA NEW GUINEA

■ Port Moresby

160°E

SOLOMON ISLANDS

■ Honiara

Darwin

INDIAN OCEAN

Cairns

Townsville

VANUATU

■ Port Vila

Broome   Tennant Creek

Mount Isa

Rockhampton

NEW CALEDONIA (Fr.)

■ Noumea

20°S

Alice Springs

A U S T R A L I A

Brisbane

Tropic of Capricorn

Kalgoorlie

Cunnamula   Gold Coast

PACIFIC OCEAN

Perth

Port Augusta

Newcastle

Sydney
Wollongong
■ Canberra

Adelaide

Albany

N

Melbourne

Auckland

Hamilton

NEW ZEALAND

SOUTHERN OCEAN

Hobart

Greymouth

■ Wellington

Christchurch

Dunedin

40°S

120°E   140°E   160°E   180°

Fact box

▲	**area:**	8 564 421km²
▲	**highest point:**	Mount Wilhelm 4 509m
▼	**lowest point:**	Lake Eyre 16m below sea level
	longest river:	River Murray-Darling 3 750km

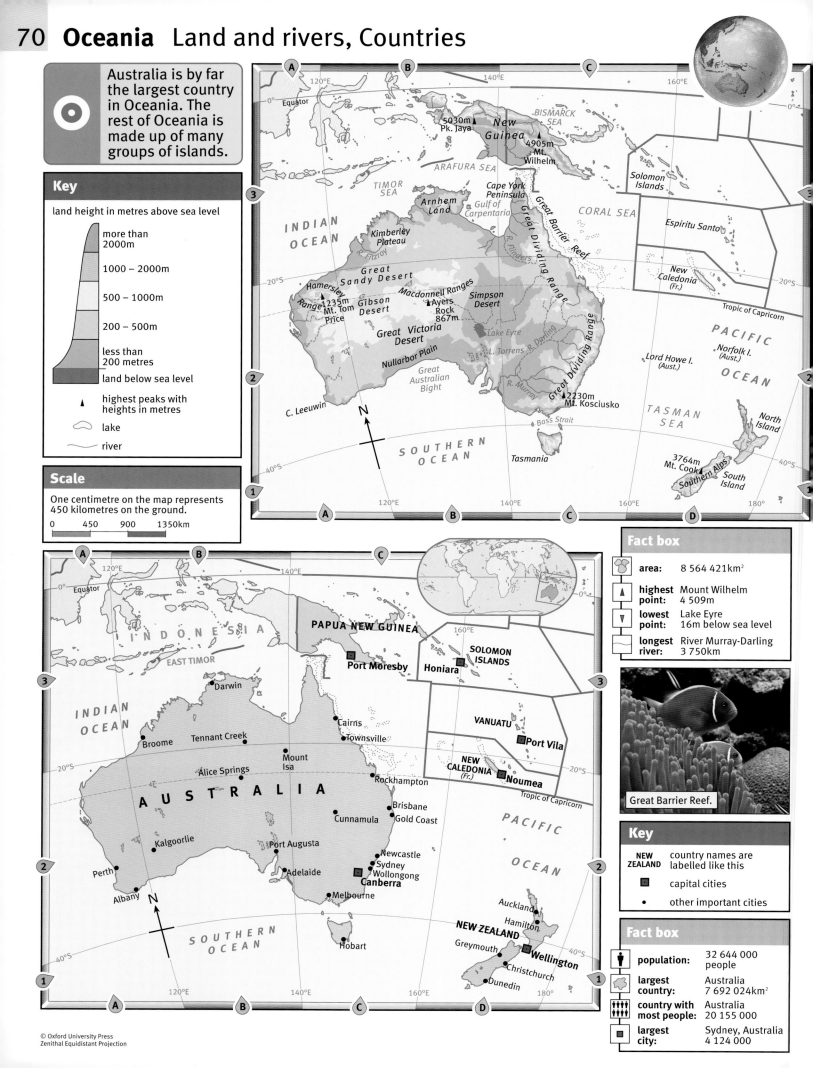

Great Barrier Reef.

Key

NEW ZEALAND — country names are labelled like this

■ capital cities

• other important cities

Fact box

	population:	32 644 000 people
	largest country:	Australia 7 692 024km²
	country with most people:	Australia 20 155 000
	largest city:	Sydney, Australia 4 124 000

New Zealand has mountains, volcanoes, glaciers and fiords. Its varied landscapes make the country a popular location for films.

North Cape
Whangarei
Dargaville
Kaipara Harbour
Great Barrier Island
Hauraki Gulf
Auckland
Bay of Plenty
Hamilton
Tauranga
Whakatane
East Cape
North Island
R. Waikato
Rotorua
Lake Taupo
Taupo
New Plymouth
Gisborne
R. Wanganui
Hawke Bay
Hawera
Napier
Hastings
Wanganui
Cape Farewell
Palmerston North
Levin
Tasman Bay
Masterton
Nelson
Cook Strait
Wellington
Westport
River Wairau
Blenheim
Greymouth
South Island
SOUTHERN ALPS
Canterbury Plains
Pegasus Bay
Christchurch
Ashburton
3764m Mt. Cook
Canterbury Bight
Timaru
Lake Wakatipu
R. Waitaki
Milford Sound
Queenstown
Oamaru
Lake Te Anau
R. Clutha
Gore
Dunedin
Invercargill
Foveaux Strait
Southwest Cape
Stewart Island

TASMAN SEA

NEW ZEALAND

SOUTH PACIFIC OCEAN

Key

▬▬▬	country boundary
▬ ▬ ▬	disputed boundary
▬▬	motorway or main road
—	railway
⊕	main airport
∿	river
⬭	lake

towns and cities

■	capital cities
○	largest towns
•	other large towns

land height

above sea level in metres

more than 5000m
2000 – 5000m
1000 – 2000m
500 – 1000m
200 – 500m
less than 200 metres
land below sea level

▲ highest peaks with heights in metres

Scale

One centimetre on the map represents 75 kilometres on the ground.

0   75   150   225km

Locator

What is the name of the water that separates North Island and South Island ? **?**

© Oxford University Press
Conical Orthomorphic Projection

The kiwi is the national symbol of New Zealand.

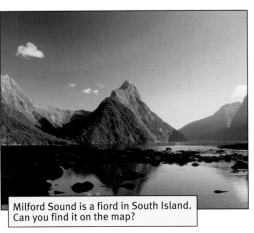

Milford Sound is a fiord in South Island. Can you find it on the map?

Rotorua, North Island, is known for its hot springs and hot mud pools.

Key

——	country boundary
- - -	state boundary
——	motorway or main road
——	railway
⊕	main airport
～	river
⌢	lake

land height
above sea level in metres

- more than 5000m
- 2000 – 5000m
- 1000 – 2000m
- 500 – 1000m
- 200 – 500m
- less than 200 metres
- land below sea level
- ▲ highest peaks with heights in metres

towns and cities

- ▣ capital cities
- ○ largest towns
- • other large towns

Scale

One centimetre on the map represents 150 kilometres on the ground.

0   150   300   450km

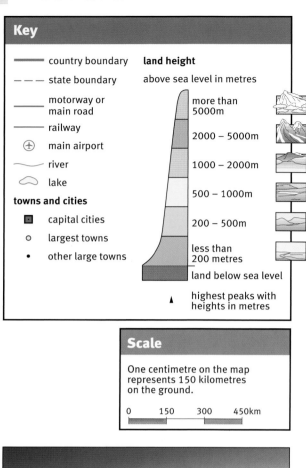
Uluru is sacred to the Aborigine people of Australia. It is also called Ayers Rock.

Sheep stations are where sheep are raised for wool and meat. They can be thousands of square kilometres in size.

Sydney is the largest city in Australia and the capital of New South Wales.

Most Australians live near the coast. The vast inland region is hot and dry and much of it is desert.

© Oxford University Press
Zenithal Equidistant Projection

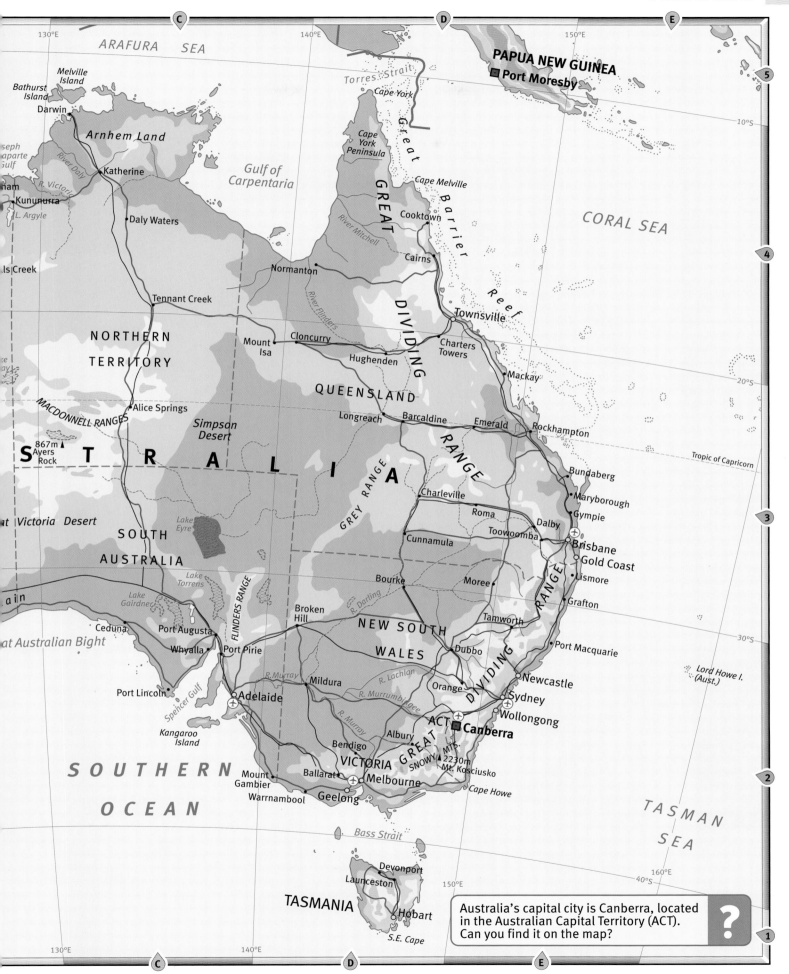

ARAFURA SEA

PAPUA NEW GUINEA
◼ **Port Moresby**

130°E

140°E

150°E

Torres Strait

Cape York

Melville Island

Bathurst Island

Darwin

Arnhem Land

seph aparte Gulf

R. Victoria

Katherine

Kununurra

L. Argyle

ham

Daly Waters

Cape York Peninsula

Cape Melville

Gulf of Carpentaria

Cooktown

River Mitchell

Cairns

CORAL SEA

10°S

ls Creek

Tennant Creek

Normanton

River Flinders

GREAT

Townsville

BARRIER

Reef

NORTHERN

TERRITORY

Mount Isa

Cloncurry

Charters Towers

Hughenden

Mackay

DIVIDING

Alice Springs

MACDONNELL RANGES

867m ▲ Ayers Rock

S

QUEENSLAND

Longreach

Barcaldine

Emerald

Rockhampton

20°S

Simpson Desert

T

R

A

L

I

A

RANGE

Bundaberg

Tropic of Capricorn

ke

ay

SOUTH AUSTRALIA

Lake Eyre

Victoria Desert

GREY RANGE

Charleville

Roma

Maryborough

Gympie

Dalby

Toowoomba

Brisbane

3

Cunnamula

Lake Torrens

Bourke

Moree

Gold Coast

Lismore

DIVIDING RANGE

Grafton

at Australian Bight

Lake Gairdner

FLINDERS RANGE

R. Darling

Tamworth

Ceduna

Port Augusta

Broken Hill

NEW SOUTH

Port Macquarie

30°S

Whyalla

Port Pirie

WALES

Dubbo

Lord Howe I. (Aust.)

Port Lincoln

Spencer Gulf

R. Murray

Mildura

R. Lachlan

Orange

Newcastle

R. Murrumbidgee

Sydney

Adelaide

Wollongong

Kangaroo Island

R. Murray

ACT ◼ **Canberra**

Albury

SOUTHERN

Bendigo

GREAT

SNOWY MTS. ▲ 2230m Mt. Kosciusko

2

Mount Gambier

Ballarat

VICTORIA

Melbourne

Cape Howe

OCEAN

Warrnambool

Geelong

TASMAN

SEA

Bass Strait

160°E

Devonport

Launceston

150°E

40°S

TASMANIA

Hobart

S.E. Cape

130°E

140°E

C

D

E

Australia's capital city is Canberra, located in the Australian Capital Territory (ACT). Can you find it on the map?

?

1

◎ The Arctic Ocean is mostly covered with frozen water.

Key

- ice cap
- sea covered by ice all year
- ▲ highest peaks with heights in metres
- ⊕ position of magnetic north in 2008
- ■ capital cities

Scale

One centimetre on the map represents 400 kilometres on the ground.

0   400   800   1200km

Fact box

area: 14 200 000km²

depth of the ocean at the North Pole: 4 087m

Icebergs are large pieces of ice that have broken off the ice shelf and float on the sea. Most of the iceberg is under water.

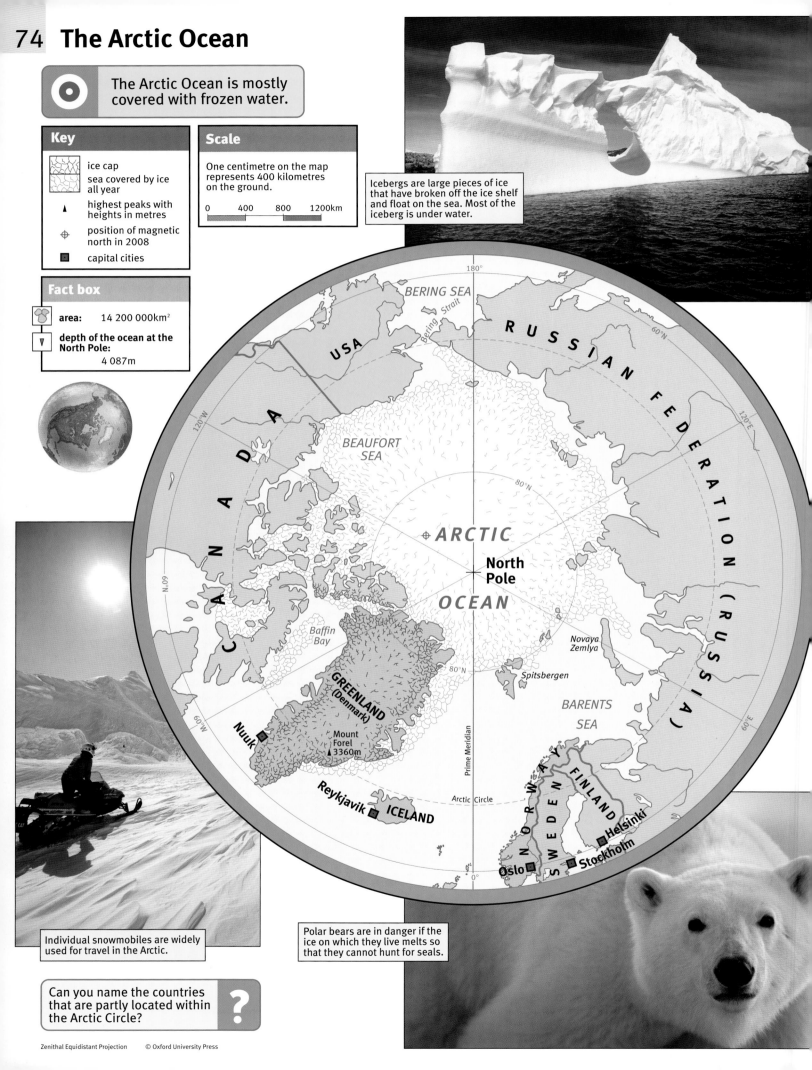

BERING SEA

Bering Strait

USA

RUSSIAN FEDERATION (RUSSIA)

60°N

C A N A D A

BEAUFORT SEA

120°W

120°E

80°N

⊕ ARCTIC

North Pole

OCEAN

90°N

Baffin Bay

80°N

Novaya Zemlya

Spitsbergen

GREENLAND (Denmark)

BARENTS SEA

60°W

60°E

Nuuk ■

Mount Forel ▲3360m

Prime Meridian

Reykjavik ■ ICELAND

Arctic Circle

N O R W A Y

S W E D E N

F I N L A N D

Helsinki ■

Oslo ■   Stockholm ■

0°

Individual snowmobiles are widely used for travel in the Arctic.

Polar bears are in danger if the ice on which they live melts so that they cannot hunt for seals.

Can you name the countries that are partly located within the Arctic Circle? ?

Zenithal Equidistant Projection

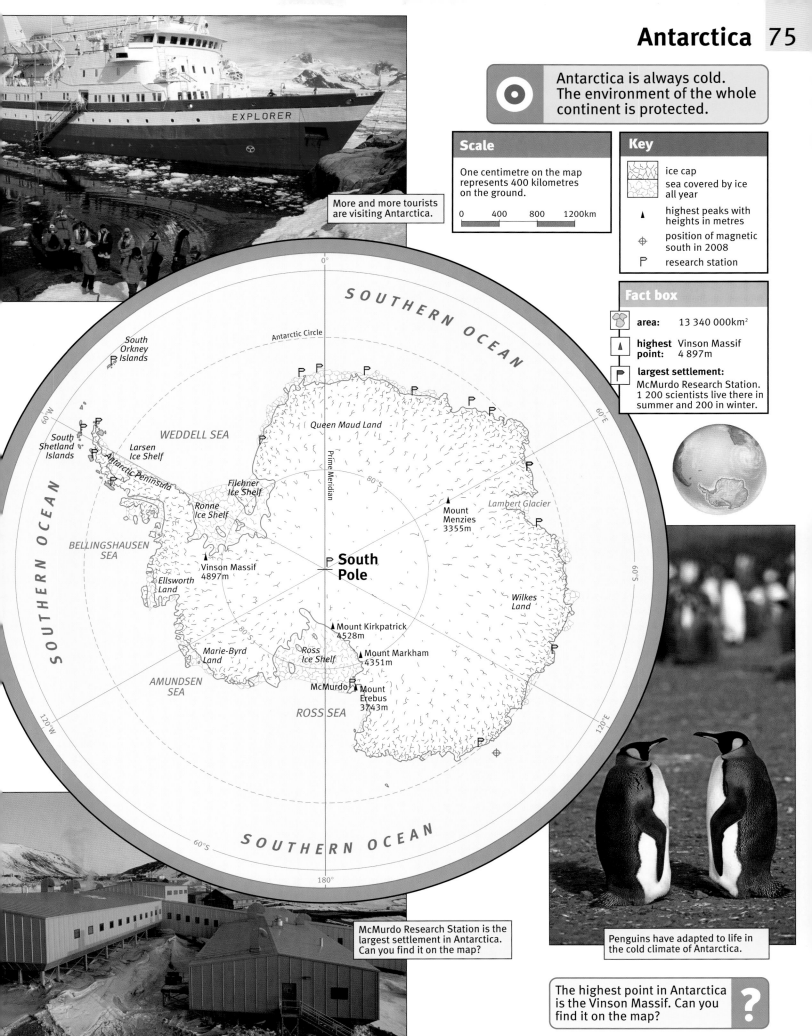

More and more tourists are visiting Antarctica.

Antarctica is always cold. The environment of the whole continent is protected.

Scale

One centimetre on the map represents 400 kilometres on the ground.

0   400   800   1200km

Key

	ice cap
	sea covered by ice all year
▲	highest peaks with heights in metres
⊕	position of magnetic south in 2008
P	research station

Fact box

area: 13 340 000km²

highest point: Vinson Massif 4 897m

largest settlement: McMurdo Research Station. 1 200 scientists live there in summer and 200 in winter.

SOUTHERN OCEAN

South Orkney Islands

Antarctic Circle

0°

South Shetland Islands

WEDDELL SEA

Queen Maud Land

Antarctic Peninsula

Larsen Ice Shelf

Filchner Ice Shelf

Ronne Ice Shelf

BELLINGSHAUSEN SEA

Vinson Massif 4897m

Ellsworth Land

SOUTHERN OCEAN

Prime Meridian

80°S

South Pole

Mount Menzies 3355m

Lambert Glacier

Wilkes Land

60°E

Mount Kirkpatrick 4528m

Marie-Byrd Land

Ross Ice Shelf

Mount Markham 4351m

AMUNDSEN SEA

McMurdo

Mount Erebus 3743m

ROSS SEA

120°W

120°E

60°S

60°S

60°W

SOUTHERN OCEAN

60°S

180°

McMurdo Research Station is the largest settlement in Antarctica. Can you find it on the map?

Penguins have adapted to life in the cold climate of Antarctica.

The highest point in Antarctica is the Vinson Massif. Can you find it on the map? **?**

Zenithal Equidistant Projection   © Oxford University Press

Country data files

Choose two countries. Using the information on these pages, can you say how your countries are the same and how they are different? **?**

Country — area in square kilometres	Population — estimated number of people in 2009 — 👤 represents 10 million people	Family size — number of children in an average family — 👤 one child / Years of life — number of years people can expect to live — 🕯 represents 10 years	Work — if there were 100 people in the country, this is where they would work — 👤 farms — 👤 factories — 👤 offices and services	Rich and poor — the average amount each person spends in a year, converted into US dollars — 💰 $1000 — 💰 $500 / Health — the number of doctors for every 10 000 people — 👤 one doctor
Australia 7 741 000km²	👤👤 21 852 000 people	2 children / 🕯🕯🕯🕯🕯🕯🕯🕯 81 years		$37 250 / 25 doctors
Brazil 8 547 000km²	👤👤👤👤👤👤👤👤👤👤👤👤👤👤👤👤👤👤👤 191 481 000 people	2 children / 🕯🕯🕯🕯🕯🕯🕯 73 years		$10 008 / 12 doctors
China 9 598 000km²	1 331 398 000 people	1.6 children / 🕯🕯🕯🕯🕯🕯🕯 73 years		$6010 / 14 doctors
India 3 288 000km²	1 171 029 000 people	2.7 children / 🕯🕯🕯🕯🕯🕯 64 years		$2930 / 6 doctors
Kenya 580 000km²	👤👤👤👤 39 070 000 people	4.9 children / 🕯🕯🕯🕯🕯 54 years		$1560 / 1 doctor

© Oxford University Press

| Country area in square kilometres | Population estimated number of people in 2009 — 👤 represents 10 million people | Family size number of children in an average family — 👤 one child — Years of life number of years people can expect to live — 🕯 represents 10 years | Work if there were 100 people in the country, this is where they would work — 👤 farms — 👤 factories — 👤 offices and services | Rich and poor the average amount each person spends in a year, converted into US dollars — 💰 $1000 — 💰 $500 — Health the number of doctors for every 10 000 people — 👤 one doctor |

Nigeria
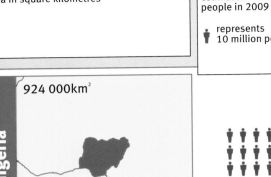
924 000km²
152 616 000 people
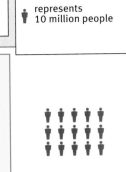
5.7 children
47 years
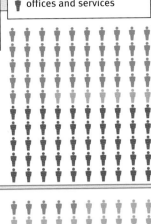
💰💰 $1980
👤👤👤 3 doctors

Spain
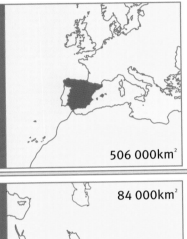
506 000km²
46 916 000 people
1.5 children
81 years
$30 830
33 doctors

United Arab Emirates
84 000km²
5 066 000 people
2.0 children
77 years
$55 200
20 doctors

United Kingdom
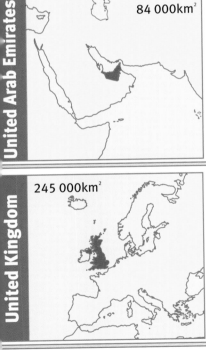
245 000km²
61 823 000 people
1.9 children
79 years
$36 240
23 doctors

USA
9 364 000km²
306 805 000 people
2.1 children
78 years
$46 790
26 doctors

name of place   grid code

London **31** C2

page number